Jeffrey A. Ryan
Nov. 3, 2001

WHOLESOME READING DISTRIBUTED BY
CHOICE BOOKS
9920 ROSEDALE M.C. RD.
IRWIN, OHIO 43029
614-857-1368
WE WELCOME Y

D0948094

Is somethir st naggi Holding you back?

Literally thousands of today's adults have something in
their past that nags at them . . .
    haunts them with guilt . . .
        taunts them with bad memories . . .
            oppresses them with spiritual defeat.

You may be one of them. Struggling to overcome a
stubborn habit. Or to erase a bad memory.

Today, you can turn trauma into triumph.

In this breakthrough book, the bestselling author of **How
to Say No to a Stubborn Habit** gives you the steps to
freedom that have worked for hundreds of men and
women he has counseled in his personal ministry.

You'll find practical, proven help for overcoming the pain
and guilt of haunting memories and addictions. You'll
learn the secret of . . .

Putting Your Past Behind You

Erwin W. Lutzer

Putting Your Past Behind You

Here's Life Publishers

First Printing, August 1990
Second Printing, January 1991
Third Printing, November 1991

Published by
HERE'S LIFE PUBLISHERS, INC.
P. O. Box 1576
San Bernardino, CA 92402

Library of Congress Cataloging-in-Publication Data
Lutzer, Erwin W.
    Putting your past behind you : turn yesterday's trauma into today's
triumph / Erwin W. Lutzer.
        p.   cm.
    Includes bibliographical references.
    ISBN 0-89840-290-5
    1. Christian life—1960- . 2. Spiritual healing. 3. Consolation. I. Title.
BV4501.2.L893   1990b
248.8'6—dc20   90-41771
                                                                    CIP

    Unless otherwise indicated, Scripture quotations are from *The New American
Standard Bible,* © The Lockman Foundation 1960, 1962, 1963, 1968, 1971, 1972,
1975, 1977.
    Other Scripture quotations are from the *King James Version* (KJV) and the
New International Version (NIV).

Cover photography by Steve Marts/AllStock
Cover design by David Marty Design

For More Information, Write:
L.I.F.E.—P.O. Box A399, Sydney South 2000, Australia
Campus Crusade for Christ of Canada—Box 300, Vancouver, B.C., V6C 2X3, Canada
Campus Crusade for Christ—Pearl Assurance House, 4 Temple Row, Birmingham, B2 5HG, England
Lay Institute for Evangelism—P.O. Box 8786, Auckland 3, New Zealand
Campus Crusade for Christ—P.O. Box 240, Raffles City Post Office, Singapore 9117
Great Commission Movement of Nigeria—P.O. Box 500, Jos, Plateau State Nigeria, West Africa
Campus Crusade for Christ International—Arrowhead Springs, San Bernardino, CA 92414, U.S.A.

I affectionately dedicate this book
to Lori
our first gift from God
who loves books and delights in words
and most especially
God's book and God's words.

I have more insight than all my teachers,
For Thy testimonies are my meditation (Psalm 119:99).

CONTENTS

INTRODUCTION

Finding a Way Out of the Cave

JOHN BRADSHAW, in *Healing the Shame That Binds You*, tells a parable of a prisoner in a cave:

There once was a man who was sentenced to die. His captors blindfolded him and marched him into a pitch-dark cave about a hundred yards square. He was told there was a way out of the cave, and if he could find it, he would be a free man.

After being put into the cave, he was free to take his blindfold off and roam in the darkness. He would be fed only bread and water for the first thirty days and nothing thereafter. The bread and water were lowered from a small hole (about a foot in diameter) in the roof at the south end of the cave. The ceiling was about eighteen feet high. The prisoner could see a faint light up above, but no light came into the cave.

As the prisoner crawled around the cave, he bumped into a number of rocks, some of which were rather large. He thought, *If I can build a mound of rocks and dirt that is high enough, I can reach the opening and enlarge it enough to crawl through and escape.* Since he was about six feet tall and he could comfortably reach another two feet, he figured the mound would have to be at least ten feet high.

He spent his waking hours collecting rocks and digging up dirt. At the end of two weeks he had built a mound about six feet high. He thought, *If I can duplicate that in the next two weeks, I can make it through the hole before my food runs out.*

By now he already had used most of the rocks, so he continued digging dirt with his bare hands. When the month had passed the mound was still less than nine feet high. He was exhausted and weak, but he thought he still might be able to reach the opening by jumping.

On the thirtieth day he climbed the mound, and he jumped. Unfortunately, his jump was short and he fell down the side of the mound. He was too weak to get up and in two days he died.

When his captors opened the cave to retrieve his body, the light of the sun illuminated an opening in the wall that led into a tunnel. This tunnel led to the other side of the mountain—the passage to freedom he had been told about. If he had found the tunnel and crawled 200 feet, he would have gained his freedom. He had *focused so completely on the small opening of light that it never occurred to him to look for freedom anywhere else.* Liberation was available, but it was concealed in the darkness.

Maybe you likewise are seeking an exit from the darkness, the darkness of your past, but you are frustrated because progress is too slow, perhaps even imperceptible. You are weary of digging and piling up stones for a ladder to escape your prison. You have been doing it by yourself, possibly with encouragement from others, but you are ready to give up.

Perhaps in the night of your experience you have missed something. Though the walls of your cave appear solid and formidable, I promise you there is a way out of the darkness. Light can come to your heart; your soul can be at rest.

Isaiah predicted that when Christ would come, the gloom would dissipate:

> The people who walk in darkness
> will see a great light;
> Those who live in a dark land;
> The light will shine on them (9:2).

Christ is the light who guides us out of the darkness of our past. How easy it is to overlook the promises He gave to His people: "You shall know the truth, and the truth shall make you free" (John 8:32); and, "Peace I leave with you; My peace I give to you; not as the world gives, do I give to you. Let not your heart be troubled, nor let it be fearful" (John 14:27).

Turning to Christ for emotional and spiritual healing will be dismissed as too simplistic by many who are determined to find their answers elsewhere — in personality theories, the techniques of humanistic psychotherapy, or a myriad of self-help remedies. I fear that, in the end, these may be about as helpful as building a pile of rocks from which to climb out of a small hole in the roof of a cave.

To aggressively apply the principles of Scripture does not mean our past can be put behind us in one act of submission to God. What it does mean is that Christ walks with us into the caves of our past and brings the hidden things to light. Then He gives us the grace to put them behind us so we can climb into the sunshine.

As you read this book , try to keep these principles clearly in mind:

1. Healing of past wounds is a process, a journey — not an event; and Christ promises that He is with you the whole way.

2. Choosing Christ as your therapist does not mean that only the two of you are needed to put your past behind you. Christ is on earth today through His people, and part of the healing process always involves other members of the body of Christ who stand ready to listen to you, cry with you, and pray for you.

3. When God puts your past behind you, it does not mean you will never be influenced by it again. Decisions made years ago will still affect you; the treatment you received from others will still leave

some scars. What it does mean is that you will be free in your own souls . . . free to love and trust, and free to be and do what God desires.

I've heard it said that people are only as sick as their darkest secrets. This book is written with the hope that you will be able to confront your own secrets and then lay them to rest.

After a discussion of the basic principles, this book concludes with some actual testimonies, true stories of people who put their dreadful pasts behind them. No matter what you face today, you can be assured that someone, somewhere, has had a similar background and has faced it successfully.

"God loves us the way we are," someone observed, "but He loves us too much to leave us that way!" Change is always possible.

There is a way out of the cave. Though it may begin in darkness, eventually it will lead to light.

1

LIVING WITH A TATTOO

It's never too late for new beginnings

ONE DAY I MET A WOMAN with a tattoo on her arm. She explained to me, "My former boyfriend did it—he was an abusive alcoholic." She was now happily married to another man, but every day she was reminded of the pain in her past. She would have given anything to remove it, but at that time, the tattoo was there to stay.

I have met people whose past is tattooed onto their souls. They've experienced abuse, lived in immorality, or acquired addictions. Some are women who live with the memory of an abortion; others are men who have fathered children out of wedlock. On today's news I heard of a young woman who turned her own father over to authorities because she had watched him commit a murder when she was a child. Think of the memories tattooed onto her soul!

How different our past would be if we could relive it, knowing what we know now. Louisa Tarkington expressed the wish of millions when she wrote:

> I wish there were some wonderful place
> Called the Land of Beginning Again,
> Where all of our past mistakes and heartaches,
> And all of our poor selfish grief,
> Could be dropped like a shabby old coat
> At the door
> And never be put on again.

Is there such a place? I believe there is.

True, we cannot go back in time and begin again, for hours become days, days become months, and months become years that can never be relived. No one can go back to the starting line in the race of life. Tacking an old calendar on the wall will not bring back the years to allow us to erase imprints left by decisions and mistakes of bygone days. We cannot go to God, as one teenager did, with, "Lord, I pray this accident might not have happened!"

Like holes left in a wall after nails have been removed, the gaping wounds of sin often leave ugly sores. These need to be bandaged and treated with ointment so they can heal.

Yes, we can have a new beginning. God wants to take our open wounds and heal them. Wounds can become battle scars that prove healing has taken place. Guilt, regret and heartache can be put behind us—there is a land of beginning again. Our past need not control our present or future. It is never too late to do what is right, never too late to live our remaining days for God.

In *The Scarlet Letter,* Nathaniel Hawthorne tells the story of a woman who has a love affair with a young minister. As the story opens she is being punished by having to stand on a public platform with the large letter A (for "Adultery") on her breast. She holds her illegitimate son in her arms. As the story unfolds she makes public expiation for her sin, taking the insults of the townspeople as her due—but she steadfastly refuses to name the man.

In the meantime, her husband, a shrewd psychologist, pretends to befriend the man whom he suspects was the accomplice in the affair. On the pretense of being a doctor, the woman's husband makes this man squirm for years because he will not admit his guilt.

In the story, the immoral man who would not own up to his past suffered far more than the woman who faced her sin, accepting her shame and guilt. Better to come clean than to live with painful secrets that imprison the soul! If he had been willing to face his past, it could have been put behind him. In choosing to pretend he was innocent, he carried his past ever with him.

THE HOPE OF A NEW BEGINNING

In the Old Testament we can read the remarkable story of Gomer, a woman who knew only too well what it was like to live with the letter *A* stamped on her soul. Her husband Hosea, a prophet, had been commanded by God to marry a prostitute. Most Bible scholars believe she was not a harlot when he married her, but God did say, "Go take to yourself a wife of harlotry, and have children of harlotry; for the land commits flagrant harlotry, forsaking the LORD" (Hosea 1:2).

Hosea had two children by this woman, but when the third was born, the prophet became painfully aware the child was not his. He named the boy "Lo-ammi," which means "no kin of mine."

Gomer continued her life of immorality, going from one lover to another, never finding the acceptance and fulfillment she craved.

One day she fell into the hands of a man who was unable to care for her. Hosea saw her from a distance — distraught, angry, without food or clothes. Instinctively, he took some bread and wine and gave it to her slothful lover so he could take better care of his mistress!

Gomer's moral toboggan slide continued until she finally ended up in the hands of a man who had her auctioned off to the highest bidder. Men stood and gawked at this hapless slave whose beauty had long since been marred by the high cost of emotional and spiritual decadence. Hosea outbidded the other men and bought her for fifteen shekels of silver and a bushel and a half of barley.

Was Hosea irrational? What man would make such a painful sacrifice for a wife who had humiliated him by flaunting broken marriage vows and treating her children irresponsibly?

Foolish or not, Hosea brought her home knowing he could now be with his lover again. He believed their marriage still had a future. They would rekindle their early courtship.

What had inspired such hope in the prophet? He never would have pursued his immoral spouse unless he believed they could begin again. Without a new beginning, the future dies in the here and now.

God Himself had given Hosea hope when He said,

Therefore, behold, I will allure her,
Bring her into the wilderness,
And speak kindly to her.
Then I will give her her vineyards from there,
And the valley of Achor as a door of hope.
And she will sing there as in the days of her youth,
As in the day when she came up from the land of Egypt
(2:14,15).

Gomer would sing again.

And there is more to the story. Her marriage vows would be reinstated, and she would live in purity and faithful commitment to her husband:

And I will betroth you to Me forever;
Yes, I will betroth you to Me in righteousness
    and in justice,
In lovingkindness and in compassion,
And I will betroth you to Me in faithfulness.
Then you will know the LORD (2:19,20).

Eventually she would be as though she had never sinned. Spiritually speaking, her virginity would be restored. Yes, she would sing again. She would stop her running and come home where she belonged.

I'm not saying Hosea was written to give us an example of how a husband should treat a wayward wife—though God only knows how many marriages could be salvaged if the partners determined to show love even in the midst of unfaithfulness. Hosea's marriage does illustrate a point, though: No matter how far someone falls, restoration is always possible. God loves to save great sinners—even those wearing the big *A*.

Remember, no matter how deep or dark your valley, there is always a path leading out. Anyone can begin again. God specializes in difficult cases.

PERSPECTIVES FOR A NEW BEGINNING

The church in Corinth contained many believers who had been converted out of homosexuality, adultery, drunkenness and physical abuse. Paul wanted to assure them they could have a new beginning, a new life in Christ.

He wrote:

No temptation has overtaken you but such as is common to man; and God is faithful, who will not allow you to be tempted beyond what you are able, but with the temptation will provide the way of escape also, that you may be able to endure it (1 Corinthians 10:13).

This verse is good news for those who think their sordid past must control their future. It can assure you of several things:

1. You are not alone in your struggle.

Your past—no matter how painful it is to remember—is common to the human race. This does not mean everyone has had your experiences, but some people *have* come through similar circumstances, and they have done so triumphantly.

In this book you will read about those who have triumphed over such things as:

> alcoholism
> child abuse
> abortion
> homosexuality
> sexual addictions

Be assured that if these people could overcome the bondage and hurt of these problems, you can overcome your past, whatever it entails. Of that I am certain, and in this book we'll explore how you can do it.

All these experiences and a host of similar ones are common to mankind. In various forms these lifestyles have existed since the beginning of time.

If we as a believing church wish to have a healing ministry, we must give credible hope to those whose backgrounds are cluttered with addictions, immorality and/or criminal behavior. One-half of all children born this year will at some time in their growing-up years live with just one parent; others will experience the terror of having an alcoholic father or a dysfunctional mother.

These experiences are common to fallen humanity. Some people are greater sinners than others, and some have been sinned against in greater ways, but we all participate in the same human nature. Every one of us is somewhere on a continuum. To a greater or lesser degree we all have experienced the power of sin and have caved in to temptation. Or we have felt the sting of being betrayed and used. In some way, that is the experience of us all.

If I could listen to your story (and I have heard many in my lifetime), I could look at you and say that your trial, your addiction, your injustice is common to man. You are not facing your hurt alone.

If you interpret this to mean that what has happened in your past is not serious because such experiences are common, you have missed what I am saying by a country mile. The fact that emotional and spiritual hurt is common does not make it less painful. Nor does it exonerate the person who hurt you. Admitting the depth of that pain may be the first step you can take toward recovery.

My point is this:

No matter what you are facing, there is someone else in this world who has had the same past as you and he (or she) has faced it successfully and gone on to live a productive life.

One of the chains Satan uses to keep people bound to their past is secrecy. They believe their situation is unique; no one else has lived through their hell. Thus they carry within their hearts a dreaded secret, believing that if anyone else knew about what they had done, they themselves would be rejected. Secrecy becomes their spiritual tomb.

Frequently, as a pastor, I have heard people say, "I'm going to tell you something that no one else in all the world knows." Then follows a tale of abuse, sexual perversion or cruel injustice. I think to myself, *What a pity this person has had to bear his burden all alone these many years — even though his story is common to man.*

2. God is faithful.

"God is faithful, who will not allow you to be tempted beyond what you are able," wrote Paul. If I think I am going through a trial that is too much for God, I am calling His credibility into question. God's faithfulness means He is obligated not to give me more than I can handle.

The addict says, "God cannot give me anything that can match the euphoria of psychedelic drugs, illicit sexuality or alcoholism. He is no competition for the drives that control me, for the power that exhilarates me." Such a person denies God's faithfulness, and that is one reason he remains bound in his sins.

Understandably, thousands of people (yes, I am including Christians) are angry with God. After all, the argument goes, if God loved me, why did He let me get into this mess? Why was my father an alcoholic? Why do I have such a strong sex drive? Why did He let my dad abuse me, or my mother reject me? Why should I look to a God who failed me when I needed Him the most?

Thus the God who can help is held at bay. The very source of strength and understanding that is so needed is rejected. I have never met a person who has successfully overcome a difficult past who has not had to "forgive God." (Although He does not need forgiveness, we sometimes think He does!) A former homosexual told me he never had a partner who wasn't angry with God. They are angry because they believe this is the way God made them. This is the card they were dealt.

No one can put his past behind him until he resolves his anger against God. To understand His sovereign control over the world and yet to believe He is loving is difficult. An abused woman put it to me simply, "God wasn't there for me when I was a child; why should I think He will be there for me as an adult? *I can never trust Him!*" Yet trust Him she must if she is to have rest in her soul.

How can such anger be dissolved? We must be honest in expressing to Him exactly how we feel. I've met people who think God would send a lightning bolt out of heaven and strike them dead if they were to tell Him they feel hurt or betrayed. So rather than confront Him, they ignore Him, stuffing their hostility into their souls like garbage into a bag. The smoldering anger is stored away until it becomes unbearable. Some go to their graves in silent but seething bitterness.

David had a better solution. He would pour out his soul to God, openly admitting his disappointments and anger. He did it reverently, of course, but he did it honestly.

> Will the Lord reject forever?
>   And will He never be favorable again?
> Has His lovingkindness ceased forever?
>   Has His promise come to an end forever?
> Has God forgotten to be gracious?
>   Or has He in anger withdrawn His compassion?
> Then I said, "It is my grief,
>   That the right hand of the Most High has changed"
>   (Psalm 77:7-10).

In numerous passages David questions God, asks why the Almighty has hidden His face, and confesses confusion and disappointment with his Lord. God did not rebuke him for such direct communication. It would have been worse if David had not talked to God at all. The Almighty is well able to take the heat—even if it is not deserved.

Since God knows what we think about Him, why not say it? It's not exactly new information to Him! Festering bitterness can be siphoned off only by honest communication. Whenever we are honest with God, we end up having His grace poured into our souls.

If the first chain that ties us to our past is *secrecy,* the second is *hostility.* Anger toward God and others makes us stay in our own prisons. It causes our hearts to turn to stone. It poisons all of our relationships. Yet God is faithful. You can tell Him everything, and He will keep it a secret. The chains of the past can be broken.

3. There is a way of escape.

To bear raw pain is so excruciating that we all seek some route of escape that will make life manageable. By nature we try to dodge our painful past so we don't have to face it. Initially, this seems like the easiest route, but in the end it is much more difficult. As we shall see, God's way of escape is quite different from ours.

Here are some of our false escape routes:

DENIAL

Victims of child abuse often resort to denial to avoid the pain of reality. Children develop happy fantasies to compensate for the pains of real life. Although this is a very natural response to such trauma, eventually the past will have to be faced. Denial is never a permanently satisfying way of putting our past behind us.

Abusers resort to denial too, but for reasons different from those of their victims. They cannot bear to face what they have done. Abusive, overbearing parents, for example, find it almost impossible to face their sins and crimes. If, in later years, their children confront them with the pain they inflicted, the chances are pretty high they will deny it. Approximately 80 percent of abusive parents refuse to own up to their sins (and crimes) when confronted. They cannot bear the pain of facing reality. Various denial mechanisms are set in motion enabling them to continue their rationalizations and to substitute dreams for reality.

Alcoholics are masters of denial; they tell themselves they are not really alcoholics because they did quit drinking for several weeks. They convince themselves they are in control of their lives. They play a hundred manipulative games to get themselves off the hook. They cannot bear to see themselves as God and others see them.

COMPULSIVE BEHAVIOR

Some people cram their lives with activity — often needless activity — simply because they cannot live with themselves. They compulsively over-eat, over-

spend, or over-schedule. To deaden the pain of
loneliness and emotional emptiness, many resort
to illicit sexual relationships and destructive
friendships.

DRUGS OR ALCOHOL

Almost daily the media tells us about someone
who died of an overdose of drugs. What is forgotten
are the tens of thousands of addicts who die slowly,
bit by bit, day by day.

Alcohol is of course America's most common
form of escape. With more than ten million alcoholics in our nation, we have had much practice
in the debilitating act of escapism.

These are some of the false ways of escape courted
by the world. To embark on these paths is to perpetuate
the power of the past rather than defeat it.

What is God's true way of escape?

God's way of escape takes many forms depending
on the situation, but it always has these characteristics:

HONESTY

The acting must end. The lies that have covered
the sin must be exposed. God will deal with us only
on the basis of truth, not evasion.

Honesty is also necessary for those who have
been the victims of other people's sins. No one can
close the door to his past without taking a look at it
and "making peace" with all that is there.

HUMILITY

To be willing to do anything that God requires,
even sharing our past with some of our friends who
can pray for us in our need, is necessary. There are
times when we cannot put our past behind us
alone; we need the assistance of others.

DEALING WITH THE PAIN

Yes, the divine surgeon wants to lance our wounds so the poison can be released and healing can take place. Some wounds are too deep or the healing scab has been scraped back too many times, and surgery becomes necessary. A large area has to be cut out so that it can heal as a clean wound.

Some people have been able to put a painful past behind them rapidly, perhaps at the moment of conversion. Others have needed more time but have not had to recall all the hurt they experienced. Some others, however, will never be at peace until they have carefully looked at their past and dealt with all the hurts, one at a time.

So what is the way of escape?

It is through matching the power of God with the deepest level of human need.

The way to healing is to escape to God and His grace. Someone has said that when God closes a door, He opens a window. And when He gives you a trial, He gives you the shoulders to bear it.

I don't want to proclaim a God who is capable only of delivering people from small sins or healing those who come from slightly imperfect backgrounds. God is able to bring anyone up from the miry clay, set their feet upon a rock, and establish their foundations.

THE SEARCH FOR A NEW BEGINNING

Let's sketch the big picture, get a glimpse of our predicament, and look at the first step needed to put the past behind us and get on with living productively for God.

When Thoreau, the naturalist, was close to death he was visited by a pious aunt who asked, "Henry, have you made your peace with God?"

"I didn't know we had quarreled," he replied.

Thoreau was as far from the truth as one could ever travel. All of us have had our quarrel with God. Our problem is that we don't want to admit we've quarreled and that in the end He is always the winner.

For starters, we are born into this world under the condemnation of sin. Unfair? Think of it this way: If you were born into a family that was greatly in debt, those debts would be passed on to you even though you had not personally incurred them. When Adam sinned, we all sinned with him — we participated in his decision in the sense that he, as the father of the human race, represented all of us.

That is only the beginning of our problem. As we grow older we begin to behave like the sinners we are. The idea that evil is something we do because of the bad examples around us, and not because of the fundamental flaw within us, is naive and contrary to experience.

As we grow into adulthood our behavior patterns become solidified, and if we have few inner restraints, we tend to follow our desires wherever they lead. This begins a cycle of behavior that we simultaneously love and hate.

Most people think the solution to their predicament rests with themselves. They may swear off their old habits, or even join a self-help group, and notice some dramatic improvements. Though these changes are good, they can ultimately do harm because they become a substitute for God's answer to their dilemma. The good has become the enemy of the best.

Why? Because self-improvement cannot rectify our quarrel with God. Self-improvement cannot take away the guilt that accompanies sinful behavior; it can only redirect it. Thus guilt reappears under different labels. Too often it is pushed into the subconscious. What is God's answer to our sinfulness?

The question can be asked in many different ways but its essence is the same: How can a sinner become just before God? Christ's death on the cross was a sacrifice for sin. This means God is able to actually credit us with the righteousness of Christ. "He made Him who knew no sin to be sin on our behalf, that we might become the righteousness of God in Him" (2 Corinthians 5:21).

God is not waiting, ready to clobber wayward sinners who are brought kicking and screaming into His kingdom. We've all heard of earthly fathers who can hardly wait to whip their children into line, but our heavenly Father invites sinners to dinner, binds up their wounds and pours grace into their souls. Like the father of the prodigal, our Father in heaven calls for the best robe (a symbol of honor), the shoes (a symbol of acceptance), and the fatted calf (a symbol of fellowship). He waits for sinners not with a club but with a cup of mercy and grace.

The good news is that this act of God clears our record once for all. He declares us as righteous as Christ:

> Truly, truly, I say to you, he who hears My word, and believes Him who sent Me, has eternal life, and does not come into judgment, but has passed out of death into life (John 5:24).

This gift of righteousness is not given to everyone but is limited to those who admit their own helplessness and transfer all of their trust to Christ alone.

Is that the end of the story? If God accepts us on the basis of Christ's merit, do we ever have to confess our sins again? And does this mean we can sin as much as we please? What about those tattoos still branded onto the soul? Some are of our own making; others have been inflicted on us. Is there really hope for a new beginning?

These and other questions will be answered in the chapters that follow.

Read on.

2

PARDON FOR THE UNPARDONABLE

The truth about God's forgiveness

"DAMN YOU! DAMN YOU!" The voice of conscience has driven many a person to an early grave. It may begin as a whisper, but eventually can blare like a megaphone, driving its victim over the brink. For some, it leads to an undefined sense of depression; for others it is a call to wanton pleasure. No pleading or logic can silence that voice that tells us we are unclean, or unworthy, or doomed to the hopelessness we know we deserve.

Why is our society so guilt-ridden? Why are so many people smothering in a blanket of condemnation, a sense of failure that drives them on to even greater failures—and hopelessness?

WHERE GUILT CAN COME FROM

First, the guilt that leads to despair often begins *early in life*. Many children know they have not lived up to their parents' expectations. Their mother and father continually remind them (often with severe discipline) that they have failed. Since a child's first understanding of who he is comes from his parents, this lack of acceptance is a tremendous blow to his self-esteem. Children who are abused assume they are simply getting what they deserve. They believe they are as bad as their parents make them out to be. *If Mom and Dad think I am that evil, I must be!* the child reasons.

Understandably, the guilt becomes overwhelming. Some children feel guilty for just being alive, and they bring that emotional burden with them into their adult life.

Second, some of us remember our *schoolteachers* expressing disapproval of our performance by failing us. Even if we did well, we knew our value depended on our report card. The result was insecurity and a feeling of worthlessness.

Third, we often disappoint *ourselves*. We make foolish decisions, fail, and commit one sin after another. We know we have betrayed our basic values and think we are unworthy hypocrites. We have the track record to prove it. More guilt.

Finally, the greatest condemnation resting on our souls is the constant realization that we have disappointed *God*. Try as we might, we intuitively know He demands even more. Our misery is compounded by our awareness that He knows our whole story. How can we ever hope to please this taskmaster? Since the possibility of perfection is the most enduring of all illusions, we are doomed to keep trying, only to keep failing.

One man said his greatest fear was to stand in line behind Mother Teresa on the Day of Judgment and overhear the Lord saying to her, "Lady, you could have done a whole lot more!"

Many people assume they will be banished from the presence of the Lord without a lot of fanfare. Like Cain, their burdens seem heavier than they can bear.

CONTINUING CONSEQUENCES OF GUILT

What does guilt do to us? William Justice describes the effects of guilt and calls it the cycle of the damned. Listen to his description:

> For every failure to live up to some "ought," there is the tendency to punish one's self in such a manner as to produce another failure! And every failure produces the response, I ought not to have failed! I stand convicted of having violated an "ought" that in turn produces the need for further punishment which results in further failure.

> Having failed, I punish myself in such a manner as to produce a further sense of failure. A cycle is complete only to begin again. I have failed to live up to some "ought" for which I feel guilty. Convicted of guilt, I feel the need to pay. To pay, I choose a method that will leave me with a sense of having failed. . . . On and on rolls the cycle downward. It may be compared to a snowball rolling down a hill, adding to its own momentum with each revolution . . . this cycle goes round and round, down and down and down, and has the potential of going on and on eternally. That is at least one aspect of hell![1]

Justice also tells of a young man who was hospitalized for heroin addiction. When asked why he was knowingly blowing his mind on drugs, the young man replied that a hospital chaplain ought to know the answer to that question without being told. The young man continued, "I feel so bad about some of the things I've done, I want to die. I don't have the guts to pick up a gun and blow my brains out, so I just do it the slow way by drugs. I feel like I ought'a have to pay for what all I've done wrong. I think most of us who are using this stuff feel the same way."

This, observed Justice, is death on the installment plan.[2]

Some pay through addiction; others pay through crime. The criminal often is doing more than simply "earning a living" by breaking the law. He is living dangerously so as to be punished. Getting caught doesn't change him.

As soon as he can, he will do it again. And again. Going unpunished may be even worse for him than being caught.

Lady Macbeth, an accomplice in the death of Duncan the King, thought her blood-stained hands could be washed clean easily. "A little water clears us of this deed," she assured her husband.

Unconvinced, he intoned, "Will all great Neptune's ocean wash this blood clean from my hand?" His own answer tells the story: "No. Rather, my hand shall make all the oceans bloody!"

Though Lady Macbeth began by thinking her guilt could be erased easily, she finally gave in to the loud protestations of a defiled conscience and cried, "Here's the smell of the blood still; all the perfumes of Arabia will not sweeten this little hand." When the mental torture became unbearable, she did what 25,000 Americans do every year — she committed suicide.

There is a feeling deep within us that sin can be forgiven only if blood is shed. Of course, this is exactly what the Bible teaches: "Without shedding of blood, there is no forgiveness." Yet, unfortunately, some people choose to shed their own in a desperate but futile attempt to pay what their conscience tells them they owe.

THE UNPARDONABLE SIN

Immorality, child abuse, rape and murder — these sins and others like them have driven their victims to the inner chambers of a personal hell. There in the darkness of their own conscience they have languished, filled with remorse, self-hatred and guilt. Their private torture drives them to conclude that their sin is unpardonable.

A man who unintentionally passed the deadly disease AIDS to his wife cursed both himself and God for his past sins that caused the initial infection. "I don't want God's forgiveness even if He would give it to me," he said angrily, "because no matter what happens I deserve to burn in hell."

He believed his sin was so great that only he could bear the weight of it. Unable to forgive himself, he saw no benefit to God's forgiveness. He thought his sin was unpardonable.

Read this letter I received from another tortured young man:

> *Last Saturday night I was tempted to commit the unpardonable sin. Ever since I found out about this sin four years ago, I was worried about committing it. Well, last Saturday night it happened: I became angry and I started cursing God and calling the Holy Spirit blasphemous and insulting names.*
>
> *Then I asked for forgiveness, but nothing seemed to go right, so I began to get even more angry, and I cursed. Do you think I got God so angry that He left me?*
>
> *I know I should give up a friendship with a man who is immersed in pornography—but I have not done it.*
>
> *I didn't sleep all night because I was so upset and so worried that I had committed this sin. Do you think Satan is making me real gloomy so that I think I have committed this sin?*

Christ did speak of an unpardonable sin, but what did He mean? What is it?

The Pharisees had seen the miracles of Christ and attributed them to Satan. Christ pointed out that their conclusion was illogical: Satan would never think of casting out his own accomplices (demons). Satan does not cast out Satan. Only a person who is stronger than Satan can cast him out.

Christ then adds:

> Therefore I say to you, any sin and blasphemy shall be forgiven men, but blasphemy against the Spirit shall not be forgiven. And whoever shall speak a word against the Son of Man, it shall be forgiven him; but whoever shall speak against the Holy Spirit, it shall not be forgiven him, either in this age, or in the age to come (Matthew 12:31,32).

I believe the unpardonable sin was that of the spiritual rulers standing between the power of God and the common people who were willing to accept Christ's miracles as legitimate. In the context of the New Testament this sin was committed by an unbelieving nation that had lost its spiritual sensitivity and determinedly rejected God's Messiah. Spiritual blindness rested upon that entire generation of Israelites (with the exception of the believers), and they were excluded from God's grace and lovingkindness in Christ.

Why was forgiveness impossible?

It is necessary to *believe* in order to be forgiven! The Pharisees who rejected Christ's credentials were excluding themselves from the kingdom of heaven by their unbelief. In trying to extinguish the light, they were becoming so hardhearted they did not desire forgiveness.

Note well that the unpardonable sin was committed only by unbelievers, that is, those who did not receive Christ for salvation. It is the natural consequence of an unbelieving heart. This sin cannot be committed in the same sense today because (1) Christ is not on the earth performing miracles to convince us that He is the Messiah, and (2) this sin was the Jews' national rejection of Christ.

Some people today, though, do commit *an* unpardonable sin through their persistent rejection of Christ.

Be assured that if you are concerned about having committed the unpardonable sin, you have not done so! Your sensitivity proves that God is working in your heart. Those who repeatedly close their lives to God may find they have no concern whatever about their relationship with

Him. Obviously, pardon is available only for those who want it.

The man who wrote the above letter must first settle the question of whether he is a Christian. If so, his next step is to repent of all sin that the Holy Spirit brings to his attention. If necessary, he also should receive counsel from mature believers who can bring him to the assurance of forgiveness. Thankfully, his sin is not unpardonable.

Yet, my friend, even as you read this chapter, you also may feel your sin is unpardonable. Or you may know someone who thinks he has crossed the line that leads to the abyss of unrelenting regret and a tortured conscience. Night settles on the soul without the promise of a sunrise.

The good news is that pardon is available and you can receive it. To help you be assured that you are forgiven, let me explain the concepts of forgiveness and grace in the New Testament.

THE PATH TO PARDON

Ponder these words:

And when you were dead in your transgressions and the uncircumcision of your flesh, He made you alive together with Him, having forgiven us all our transgressions, having canceled out the certificate of debt consisting of decrees against us and which was hostile to us; and He has taken it out of the way, having nailed it to the cross (Colossians 2:13,14).

Paul is referring to an ancient custom where the paid debts of an individual were listed on a piece of parchment with "Paid in Full" written on it. Then it was nailed on a public billboard so all could see that the debts of this man were paid.

When Christ died on the cross He took all the debts we, as lawbreakers, owed God, and He paid them. God the Father received that payment and was fully satisfied with it. Figuratively speaking, the bill that was paid was nailed to the cross for all to see.

Incredibly, as Christians we do not owe God any righteousness—Jesus met our obligations for us. His word on the cross, "It is finished," is but one word in Greek and it means "Paid in full"!

Understanding the implications of God's grace is the starting point for a clear conscience. Remember that Christ's death was payment for all we have done, *past, present* and *future*. Obviously, the sacrifice included sins that we have not yet committed. All our sins were future 2000 years ago—and these in their entirety were laid on Christ. If you are a Christian, there is no sin you will ever commit that has not *already* been paid for.

A popular misconception is that when we were saved God forgave only those sins we had committed up to that point. Then through confession we keep our salvation "up to date." If that were true, we could have no assurance of heaven. What if you or I were to die tomorrow with unconfessed sins on our conscience? Would we be lost and headed for hell?

The good news is that when we trusted Christ as our Savior, in one act God wiped all of our sins away—even the sins we have not yet committed. The text says He forgave us *all* our transgressions the moment we were saved. Those who have truly believed on Christ belong to Him forever. We are declared righteous by God because Christ's righteousness is credited to us. Yes, He already has wiped the whole slate clean, or better, He has thrown the slate away. "For by one offering He has perfected for all time those who are sanctified" (Hebrews 10:14).

This explains why you, as a Christian, cannot commit the unpardonable sin. You have been given a *carte blanche* pardon.

There is therefore now no condemnation for those who are in Christ Jesus (Romans 8:1).

And again,

Who will bring a charge against God's elect? God is the one who justifies; who is the one who condemns? Christ Jesus is He who died, yes, rather who was raised, who is at the right hand of God, who also intercedes for us (Romans 8:33,34).

At this point we must stop for a moment and catch our breath! God's grace is so overwhelming we might be tempted to misuse it. In fact, a better response would be to pause and thank God for His generosity—it prompted Him to accept us unconditionally into His family.

Quite naturally we might ask: If our future sins already have been forgiven by God, why must we confess our sins? John wrote to Christians, "If we confess our sins, He is faithful and righteous to forgive us our sins and to cleanse us from all unrighteousness" (1 John 1:9).

Our legal *standing* before God is secure even before we confess our sins. Once the righteousness of Christ has been credited to us and God has stamped "Paid in Full" across our lives, we are secure in our Father's love. Legally, all of our sins are blotted out. We have been "accepted in the beloved" (Ephesians 1:6, KJV). Now God wants our *experience* to be in line with our official standing, and confession is the means God uses to bring us back into fellowship with Him.

The sins we commit as Christians can be compared to our disobedience as children. When I was growing up I often disappointed my parents through my lack of submission to their authority. Often I was disciplined for my disobedience, but I did not lose my sonship—even when my fellowship with them was broken.

God does the same with us. If we are not willing to repent of the sin that the Holy Spirit brings to our attention, He disciplines us by allowing us to be ensnared by the consequences of that particular sin. God has His way of correcting us if we flippantly misuse His grace. Yet our of correcting us if we flippantly misuse His grace. Yet our sonship is secure; our future with God is guaranteed. Legally we stand continuously perfect in God's sight.

Many Christians are miserable simply because they are unwilling to admit their sin humbly before God so their conscience might be cleansed. They do not have to be saved again; they are just wayward children who need to get back on talking terms with their Heavenly Father.

Let me assure you it is God's desire for you to be totally free from guilt. Why should we continue to bear the condemnation for sins that Christ has already paid for? If Christ's death has allowed us to rejoice in our forgiveness, we should honor His sacrifice and do so.

DIFFICULTIES IN ACCEPTING FORGIVENESS

Why do so many Christians find it difficult to really believe that God has forgiven them? The promises of God's forgiveness are clear enough, but accepting that forgiveness is another matter. Something within us says, "It's too good to be true." Such forgiveness seems to contradict the normal patterns of life.

Let me suggest several reasons people who have been forgiven may still struggle with guilt.

First, the *continued consequences of sin* make it difficult to accept God's forgiveness.

Think of a teenage girl, pregnant as the result of an immoral relationship. She confesses her sin and is forgiven, cleansed by the Most High God—yet the consequences continue as the baby grows within her. She finds it hard to accept forgiveness because the child is a reminder of her immorality. She must learn to separate the *consequences* of sin from the *forgiveness* of sin.

The man who says he will not seek forgiveness for having given his wife AIDS but wants to burn in hell because he deserves it—that man must learn to separate forgiveness and consequences. Of course he deserves to burn in hell, just as all of us do! Yet he can be washed whiter than snow, even if his wife dies of the virus he gave her.

I am told that Ted Bundy, who died in the electric chair for killing approximately 28 young women, accepted Christ as Savior before his death. We cannot verify this for no one can know the human heart, but *it is possible that he did.* If so, he entered into the presence of God absolutely acquitted, forgiven, and cleansed by God—despite the awful continuing results of his hideous crimes.

Thankfully, God forgives sins whose consequences continue even into eternity. "As far as the east is from the west, so far has He removed our transgressions from us" (Psalm 103:12).

A **second** reason some people find it hard to accept God's forgiveness is, they *view guilt as necessary punishment.*

I've known Christians who have postponed confessing their sins, thinking it was just too easy to come to God and be instantly forgiven. Or, after confessing, they have continued to bear the guilt of their sin, insisting that they pay at least something for what they have done! That is the devil's lie.

Guilt is *not* God's punishment! God uses guilt for one purpose only and that is to lead us to Christ that we might repent of our sins and be cleansed. Guilt is God's way of reminding us we have violated His standard and must be brought back into moral agreement with Him.

Of course when we sin we should feel guilty; not to feel guilt is a sign of a hard heart. Once we have confessed those sins, though, guilt has accomplished its purpose. It is never a means of payment, never a feeling we must endure because we deserve it. Such reasoning denies the liberating truth that Christ paid our price in full. Guilt cannot add a single stroke of merit to the perfect sacrifice.

I've learned by experience that many Christians cannot distinguish the prompting of the Holy Spirit from the accusations of Satan. The difference is this: The Holy Spirit convicts us for sins that we have been unwilling to face in God's presence; Satan makes us feel guilty for sins that are already under the blood of Christ. The Holy Spirit reminds us of our sins *before* we are cleansed; Satan continues to remind us of them *after* we are cleansed.

A **third** reason we often struggle with accepting God's forgiveness is, we *cannot forgive ourselves.*

We can understand that God is gracious and merciful, but how can we make peace with ourselves?

Such reasoning is foolish. If God—the one who knows all about me, the supreme Lawgiver of the universe—has forgiven me, what right do I have to deny myself forgiveness? Do I know something about my life that He has overlooked? If the Almighty has pronounced me clean, do I have the right to pronounce myself guilty?

No matter how humble some people appear to be, the fact that they cannot forgive themselves merely indicates they have depreciated the value of Christ's sacrifice. The assumption is, they have come across a sin that was not included in Christ's death. They also are filled with enough pride to think they can atone for their own sin.

In my counseling I have discovered that most people who have never forgiven themselves have not really accepted God's forgiveness. To experience peace with God is to be at peace with oneself.

Finally, if you *intend to keep committing the same sin,* you will never feel forgiven, no matter how intense your confession.

A man may confess his sexual infidelity to God, but unless he is willing to break with this sin entirely (this almost always involves seeking counsel and the forgiveness of those he has wronged), he will not sense the release that comes with a cleansed conscience.

We find it so much easier to confess our sins to God than to make restitution. Yet when we come to God we must be honest. Being willing to do whatever we can to be reconciled with those whom we have sinned against is absolutely essential for us to experience God's forgiveness.

We may be afraid of the other person's reaction— however, we are not accountable for the attitude of others toward us. Paul delineates our responsibility: "Be kind to one another, tender-hearted, forgiving each other, just as God in Christ also has forgiven you" (Ephesians 4:32). If we have wronged others, we must make sure we seek their forgiveness. Our goal is to have a conscience void of offense toward God and toward men.

In those instances where our actions have affected others, we especially need to have the courage to deal with our sins in the presence of some other human being(s). When James wrote, "Therefore, confess your sins to one another, and pray for one another, so that you may be healed" (5:16), he was not speaking about just the healing of the body, but also the healing of the soul. Every one of us, at some time or another, must confront our past in the light of others and their response to us. We need to share our life with at least one other committed Christian who can understand the depths of our sin and yet can give us the assurance of Christ: "Neither do I condemn you, your sins are forgiven. . . . Go and sin no more" (John 8:11).

There can be no growth in the Christian life until the barrier of guilt from the past has been cleared away.

LIVING WITH THE CONSEQUENCES

Okay, you have accepted God's forgiveness and you have chosen to forgive yourself—but the consequences we have mentioned are still there, aren't they?

A mother lives with the painful memories of giving her baby away in adoption—she knows a little girl is growing up somewhere who will never know who her real mommy is. A man looks back to a life of alcoholism that drove his children away from home. A husband faces the painful fact that his affair caused a divorce he did not want and now he must live separated from his family. How do you handle these situations?

The only sensible course of action is to *give these consequences to God*. Some matters quite literally must be transferred from our hands to His. When we trust Him to make the best of the mess we have left behind, He will be gracious and display His mercy and grace.

Even weeds, growing as a result of the earth's curse, frequently are graced with beautiful flowers. Adam and Eve, who made the biggest blunder known in the universe, are clothed with the skins of animals. As it is written: "Where sin increased, grace abounded all the more" (Romans 5:26).

Thankfully, the doctrine of karma—that "unbreakable" impersonal law that says everyone gets exactly what he deserves—is a lie. The Bible assures us that God often curtails the consequences of sin, even in this life.

> He has not dealt with us according to our sins,
> Nor rewarded us according to our iniquities,
> For as high as the heavens are above the earth,
> So great is His lovingkindness toward those who fear Him
> (Psalm 103:10,11).

CONTROLLING THE MEMORIES

And what about the memories of our sin?

I counseled a woman who had had an abortion, knowing full well that she was killing her baby. It all seemed so "right" at the time, but she knew it was simply a rationalization to cover an act of immorality. When it was over, she told herself, God would surely forgive her. Now, two years later, she still cries herself to sleep, thinking of that baby whom she believes is in heaven.

Yes, she knows she is forgiven, but how does she handle the memory of that precious little baby she killed? And will this little one whom she will someday see in heaven — will that little girl ever understand?

There are days when this young woman is able to push the thoughts out of her mind, but too often they crash back into her consciousness like a dam that has just broken.

The Bible teaches that God completely blots out our sins so that He no longer remembers them:

I, even I, am the one who wipes out your transgressions
   for My own sake;
And I will not remember your sins (Isaiah 43:25).

Does that mean He is no longer omniscient? Is there really something about us He does not know? Hardly. The text simply means that God no longer has regard for our sins. He does not remind us of them; they are no longer barriers to our fellowship with Him. Someone has said that He throws our sins into the sea and then puts up a sign that reads, "No Fishing!"

This woman must forget her past sins just as God does. She will not have amnesia, for she will never forget she had an abortion — but her memories need not control her, either. She can expect those memories to come back from time to time, but they need not destroy her. God can break their power and eventually relegate them to the "no longer active" file of the mind. *What right does she have to remember what God forgets?*

And yes, in heaven, her baby will understand. God will see to it that the reconciliation is complete. He has enough grace to cover that event, too.

In a subsequent chapter we will discuss those deeper memories, the injustices done against another person — child abuse, for example — but what we must realize here is that God is greater than our past memories. The memory also can be healed.

REPAIRING THE IRREPARABLE

Satan has a vested interest in getting us to believe there are some sins for which there is no forgiveness. *The more he can magnify the horrors of our sin, the more he diminishes the value of Christ's death.* Of course sin is destructive to man and abhorrent to God, but God's remedy is equal to the task. He took into account the full extent of human need when He accepted Christ's payment.

Recently, a friend sent me this story that illustrates God's forgiveness and the fact that Satan has no right to harass us about sins God has forgiven.

In the 14th century, Robert Bruce of Scotland was leading his men in a battle to gain independence from England. Near the end of the conflict, the English wanted to capture Bruce to keep him from the Scottish crown. So they put his own bloodhounds on his trail. When the bloodhounds got close, Bruce could hear their baying. His attendant said, "We are done for. They are on your trail, and they will reveal your hiding place."

Bruce replied, "It's all right." Then he headed for a stream that flowed through the forest. He plunged in and waded upstream a short distance. When he came out on the other bank, he was in the depths of the forest. Within minutes, the hounds, tracing their master's steps, came to the bank. They went no farther. The English soldiers urged them on, but the trail was broken. The stream had carried the scent away. A short time later, the crown of Scotland rested on the head of Robert Bruce.

The memory of our sins, prodded on by Satan, can be like those baying dogs—but a stream flows, red with the blood of God's own Son. By grace through faith we are safe. No sin-hound can touch us. The trail is broken by the precious blood of Christ.

"The purpose of the cross," someone observed, "is to repair the irreparable."

3

THE BATTLE FOR YOUR MIND

*How to identify and understand the enemy,
and what weapons to use against him*

SEVERAL YEARS AGO while on a trip to Europe, my wife and I visited the Wartburg Castle in Germany, one of the largest in all of Europe. That is where Martin Luther was confined for ten months to evade capture by his enemies, and that was the time he used to translate the Bible into German.

Visualize an ancient structure of acres of heavy stone buildings within a massive wall. Imagine sentries around the top rim of the wall and a moat at its base. With no easy access to the fortress and no entrance unprotected, enemy soldiers could surround it with their horses and drawn swords but would be stopped in their tracks. Here was security at its finest.

For a moment think of your mind as a fortress, the inner chamber of the true self. In every room there is continual activity, for the inhabitants (your thoughts) are in almost perpetual, restless motion. Here strategies are discussed, decisions are made and plans are executed. Values are secretly debated, feelings are weighed, and evil and good are contemplated. Memories are either treasured or abhorred as past successes and failures make their entrance and exit. Here is the essence of your personhood, the dwelling of your soul.

Unfortunately, many adversaries struggle to gain control of the castle. Some seek to gain entrance from without; others incite rebellion from within. There is almost perpetual conflict.

Satan and his demons want to scale those walls, creating opportunities to gain influence over the human mind. When Ananias and Sapphira decided to tell a white lie, Peter later asked, "Why has Satan filled your heart to lie to the Holy Spirit?" (Acts 5:3). A thought they believed was their own actually had been injected into their minds by an evil spirit.

As for the enemies within, these are the promptings of the flesh, that sinful nature of ours that constantly vies for allegiance and control. James 4:1 asks: "What is the source of quarrels and conflicts among you? Is not the source your pleasures that wage war in your members?"

Jesus said,

For from within, out of the heart of men, proceed the evil thoughts, fornications, thefts, murders, adulteries, deeds of coveting and wickedness, as well as deceit, sensuality, envy, slander, pride and foolishness" (Mark 7:21,22).

These are the thoughts that inhabit the basement of the soul, thoughts that can be mobilized in a moment of time to war against us. These enemies within belong to the same army as the enemies without. In fact, the flesh often throws open the door of the castle and lets down the drawbridge so that the outside enemies can gain entry. Soon we find the castle invaded by powerful sinful forces determined to take up residence in the throne room.

How can we distinguish between the enemy without (demonic forces) and the enemy within (our fleshly nature)? Often we cannot, for both use the tactic of deception. Both seek to control us and eventually destroy us.

In the last chapter I spoke about the forgiveness of God—but what about the powerful temptations that seem to overwhelm us? What about a self-image that has been destroyed by past failures and injustices? Surely God has not left us to fend for ourselves!

Charles Wesley (1707-1788) understood all too well the dilemma of Christians who struggle with sins that already have been forgiven. He wrote:

> He breaks the power of cancelled sin,
> He sets the prisoner free;
> His blood can make the foulest clean;
> His blood availed for me!

The power of *cancelled* sin!

Yes, many Christians have the assurance that their sin has been cancelled, but they still come under its effects and power. Accepting spiritual freedom and tranquility of heart always involves conflict. Paul wrote:

> For though we walk in the flesh, we do not war according to the flesh, for the weapons of our warfare are not of the flesh, but divinely powerful for the destruction of fortresses. We are destroying speculations [imaginations] and every lofty thing raised up against the knowledge of God, and we are taking every thought captive to the obedience of Christ (2 Corinthians 10:3-5).

The imagination can be a good thing but it also can be the source of great evil. We read:

> Then the LORD saw that the wickedness of man was great on the earth, and that every intent of the thoughts of his heart was only evil continually (Genesis 6:5).

The most intense war we will ever face is the one for control of the mind, the battle for a wholesome imagination.

In context, Paul was speaking about the worldly wisdom the people in Corinth claimed to possess. This "wisdom" caused them to reject the wisdom of God that

Paul was trying to teach them. These speculations represent all thoughts that oppose God, and they become our enemy. Here, too, Christ is the answer. Paul says we have the weapons to tear those opposing thoughts down and bring them captive to Christ.

The solution to right living is right thinking!

Based on what Paul wrote we can outline a strategy for battle.

IDENTIFY THE ENEMY

What are those imaginations that exalt themselves against the knowledge of God? What thought patterns must be dismantled and replaced? The answer, of course, is any thoughts that are contrary to the will and purpose of God. Let me help you identify some of those destructive thoughts that even now may be playing on the video screen of your mind.

BITTERNESS

Someone has wronged you and shown no remorse. You have been misused by a friend you trusted and that person has never had the kindness even to say, "I'm sorry." Whether you like it our not, your bitterness erupts several times a day. You have tried to forgive, but it does not help much.

No matter how many times you replay the scenario in your mind, you can't find the switch to turn it off. Rehearsing what happened does not change anything; you are just as far from justice as ever. There is no sensible way you can even the score, and bitterness saps every ounce of your spiritual energy. An enemy has taken control without your explicit permission, and you don't know how to force him to leave.

SEXUAL LUST

There are no fantasies in our imaginations so strong as those of sexual temptations. The availability of sexual stimuli only intensifies the conflict. For just a few extra dollars it is possible to see a porno movie in most any hotel. Cable television has brought sexual scenes directly into the home, and even network TV continues to become increasingly explicit.

These promptings from outside the body energize those enemies already within our own souls. The tendency to rationalize, to say that everyone struggles with lust, is so powerful that some people gave up the battle for purity long ago.

Whatever the rationalization, these thoughts are a drain on our spiritual and emotional life. "Beloved, I urge you as aliens and strangers to abstain from fleshly lusts, which wage war against the soul" (1 Peter 2:11). And what a war it is!

ADDICTIONS

This topic will be considered in a later chapter, so I shall merely mention here some of the common addictions that hold power over us: alcohol, drugs, overeating, gambling, pornography, immorality, etc. These enemies destroy us by their relentless pursuit for control.

FEARFUL ATTITUDES OF DEFEAT

Children who grow up in dysfunctional homes often are overcome by shame, false guilt, and feelings of hatred toward themselves. Even some children from good backgrounds suffer from feelings of inferiority, self-doubt and fear. Living according to these attitudes aborts any possible meaning and fulfillment in our lives.

DESTRUCTIVE MEMORIES

Here we can include every kind of past experience that poisons our future. Some women have painful memories of having given up a child for adoption, or memories of rejection by their parents or an by unfaithful man. Similarly, memories of abuse, rejection or a sinful lifestyle haunt many men, and they cannot seem to find meaning to life. Guilt persistently draws our attention to the mistakes and sins of the past.

No wonder our inner conflicts are often fierce! Here we are, redeemed by God at high cost, with the Holy Spirit taking residence within us, yet plagued by every kind of sinful desire. Paul wrote: "Do you not know that your body is a temple of the Holy Spirit who is in you, whom you have from God, and that you are not your own?" (1 Corinthians 6:19). Our bodies and minds are owned by God. Yet none of the enemies we have listed will submit to His authority unless they are forced to.

How can we bring "every thought captive to the obedience of Christ" (2 Corinthians 10:5), as Paul said he was able to do in his own life? We have the same resources he had, and we can regain control even after the rebels have had free reign — but first we must understand the tactics of the enemy a bit better.

UNDERSTAND THE ENEMY

What makes the enemy seem formidable? The answer is always the same: lies, lies, lies! To the extent that we are deceived, we are overcome.

Here are some of the lies the enemy uses to get his foot in the castle door. These misbeliefs hold us hostage to destructive thoughts that work against us. Sometimes we make up the lies ourselves; at other times we accept the lies of Satan. Either way, we believe what is false, and we pay our dues.

Lie #1: *Our enemy is actually a friend.*

You may have read the list of thoughts I identified and conclude you have every right to think the way you do. You may not realize you have made peace with an enemy that will eventually ruin you.

Already I can hear a chorus of objections:

"Why should I give up my bitterness when I was the one who was wronged?"

"Why should I deny myself the pleasure of lust considering all the loneliness and hurt I feel?"

"My addiction is my crutch; it helps me get along in this painful world."

"Why should I learn to love my parents when they are the ones who ruined my life?"

If the truth were known, we would have to admit that many of us simply do not want to be free from those thought patterns that chew away at our peace of soul. We all have known the exhilaration that can come from some secret sin of the mind, some unmortified desire of the flesh. We have, at times, rationalized the pleasure, believing it was our right. To think we should give these up is like being a child and having someone threaten to take away our bag of candy.

Such rationalizations only prove the point that our enemies have duped us into believing they are our friends. We may not realize that these thoughts, these desires, seek total control — and our eventual destruction. These mental video replays neutralize our effectiveness. They leave us so defeated we cannot represent Christ in this desperate world.

When we take authority over these enemies, and they are subdued, God gives us great peace. We then wonder how we could have been so blind, so deceived.

Christ put the record straight: "The thief comes only to steal, and kill, and destroy: I came that they might have life, and might have it abundantly" (John 10:10).

Right now take a moment to identify the thought patterns that plague you. If you don't know what they are, it is unlikely you will know how to replace them with the thoughts of God.

Let's recognize our enemies! We must call them by name and realize they are not pounding on the castle door to help us but to destroy us. Only God's thoughts can give us true pleasure and peace.

Lie #2: *Our enemies' power is stronger than Christ's power.*

Lust, addiction, bitterness—these thoughts are so powerful, so overwhelming, we are tempted to believe there is no use trying to fight them. They want nothing less than our quiet resignation. The one thing our imagination detests is to have its authority questioned.

Lie #2 is just as false as lie #1. It is unthinkable that any sin would be more powerful than Christ! Charles Wesley was right—Christ does break the power of cancelled sin. There are no prison bars so strong that Christ cannot pry them apart.

To think you have to be tied to the misery caused by past sin is to bring the power of Christ into serious question. He frequently spoke about the terrible slavery of sin, but He also gave hope to the weary: "If therefore the Son shall make you free, you shall be free indeed" (John 8:36).

Of course, God has not chosen to make such spiritual freedom available without some cost in our lives. To be saved is a free gift; to live out our salvation is a daily struggle. Usually, God works on us just a bit at a time, but progress is always possible.

Lie #3: *Because of who we are and what we have done, we shall never experience God's love.*

Our society is filled with people who believe they are too sinful to merit God's love and grace. In one sense that is all too true — not a one of us merits God's mercy and love. Thankfully, He has given Himself to us in grace.

If an individual cannot receive God's love for himself, if he questions whether God loves him, he will never be able to accept human love. Every attempt others make to show kindness will be rebuffed in some way. To be spiritually productive, we must be content with the love and forgiveness of God. We must be secure in our identity as His child.

Lie #4: *We can live comfortably in two separate worlds, the inner world of thought and desires and the outer world of actions and responsibility.*

To think it is permissible to be filled with all manner of sinful thoughts as long as we do not act on them is a delusion. A woman may spend all day watching soap operas based on immorality and self interest but justify it by saying she would never do what she sees on the screen. What she doesn't understand is that we are transformed into whatever we gaze at. She becomes like the characters she imagines. As a woman thinks in her heart, so she is.

The same applies to those immersed in pornography, bitterness, anger, covetousness, etc. How skillfully we are able to hide these desires from others! How often we congratulate ourselves for being so well thought of — yet just look at our hearts!

God does not concentrate on the outward appearance. He is constantly monitoring our minds since they show the true selves. We are not what we think we are, *but what we think, we are!*

Suppose all of our thoughts (we have about 10,000 per day) were put on a clothesline, hung out to dry. There they would hang for all to see. How ashamed every one of us would be!

I doubt it would be possible for us to love one another if we could see all the thoughts we have toward each other. The pettiness, envy, anger and secret games we play would undercut any mutual respect we have. We would just want to run and hide. God does see it all, of course:

Thou hast placed our iniquities before Thee,
Our secret sins in the light of Thy presence (Psalm 90:8).

What a new understanding this gives to the love of God! He sees all that and loves us anyway. As a line of a song goes:

He who knows me best, loves me most!

To believe we can be rotten on the inside as long as we are "Christian" on the outside is deception of the worst kind. Jesus chided the Pharisees who cleaned the outside of their cup but were full of robbery and self-indulgence within (Matthew 23:25).

To gain control over our thoughts is absolutely essential for spiritual healing and progress. Eventually we must realize that, as far as God is concerned, *only the heart really matters.*

Now for some tactics to wrest the castle of the soul out of the hands of the enemy.

FIGHT THE ENEMY

We must fight the enemy with the right weapons. Notice Paul's words:

Though we walk in the flesh, we do not war according to the flesh, for the weapons of our warfare are not of the flesh, but divinely powerful for the destruction of fortresses (2 Corinthians 10:3,4).

First, *spiritual battle cannot be fought with physical weapons.*

If the enemy in your soul is anger, you cannot get rid of it by pretending a pillow is your mother-in-law and stomping on it to "get the anger out."

Lust cannot be expelled by promises to reform and determination never to buy pornography again. The Chinese students in Tiananmen Square learned you cannot stop army tanks with your bare hands. When you are fighting an enemy, your hope of victory depends on having the strongest artillery.

The weapons we use must be spiritual because the mind is a spiritual substance. Our thoughts are not matter. It would be incorrect to say, "I had a thought that was a quarter-inch long and weighed nearly one-tenth of an ounce."

The mind works in conjunction with the brain, but believe it or not, it is not necessary to have a brain in order to think! When you die, your brain disintegrates and eventually returns to dust. Yet at that moment you will be thinking more clearly than you ever have thought before, for your mind will be in heaven. D. L. Moody said, "Soon you will read in the papers that D. L. Moody is dead . . . don't believe it, for at that moment, I shall be more alive than I ever have been!"

My point is that the mind (the castle we are speaking about) is a spiritual entity, and that is why we need spiritual weapons to fight its enemy.

Second, *Satan is spiritual and thus is not deterred by physical weapons.*

There is no use thinking evil spirits can be intimidated by swords and clubs. A spiritual war must be fought with spiritual resources — we must fight spirit with spirit.

When we use the right weapons, we actually enlist the help of a power stronger than we are. We bring in reinforcements to do the job. God becomes our ally.

Since we have learned we are defeated by lies, we can understand we are rescued by truth:

> If you abide in My word, then you are truly disciples of Mine; and you shall know the truth, and the truth shall make you free (John 8:31,32).

Spiritual Weapons and Their Use

Let me list some of our spiritual weapons along with a specific application step for each so you can begin your steps to freedom.

Weapon #1: *The Death, Resurrection and Ascension of Christ*

I have already emphasized the fact that the death of Christ is the basis of our forgiveness. A lesser-known truth is that the cross is also the basis of victory over the aspirations of the flesh. Every believer must know the power of the words: "I have been crucified with Christ; and it is no longer I who live, but Christ lives in me" (Galatians 2:20a). Our old heart with its sinful desires and rebellion died when God saved us.

However, this fact cannot be applied to our lives without faith. John Piper says that sin (lust, for example) "gets its power by persuading me to believe that I will be more happy if I follow it. The power of all temptation is the prospect that it will make me happier."[1]

The only way to overcome this deception is by faith, and faith comes through dependence on God's promises. As faith builds in our hearts, we will be less apt to fall prey to the lie that the path of sin will make us the happiest. We trust the God of peace to be with us knowing that . . .

> In Thy [God's] presence is fulness of joy;
> In Thy right hand there are pleasures forever (Psalm 16:11).

Faith overcomes the dishonesty of our enemies.

Faith unleashes the power of Christ that will expose the lies and enable us to see sin for what it is. Our greatest challenge is to focus on God's Word so that faith will grow in our hearts and we will choose God's way instead of our own.

ACTION STEP:
Memorize Romans 6:1-14, asking God to build faith in your heart that sin shall no longer be your master.

Weapon #2: *The Word of Christ*

You have heard a thousand times that it is necessary to meditate on the Scriptures, but perhaps you didn't know why. As I have explained, the reason is that it will build our faith so that we can obey God with confidence, knowing that His way is best for us.

Meditation itself is a battle, for our flesh, in cahoots with Satan, will want to keep us distracted from God's truth. If we are not thinking about what we are reading, our faith will not be strengthened.

ACTION STEP:
Read a paragraph or two of Scripture before 9:00 every morning, and then answer these three questions for yourself:
  (1) What did I learn about God?
  (2) What does this passage tell me as a
      believer to do?
  (3) What thought can I take with me
      for today?

Before you dismiss this step as too simplistic, try it for at least two weeks. Without meditation in the Word of God, you will never be able to keep the enemies of the soul in check. When we neglect the Word of God for even a few days, our faith dissipates and we become vulnerable to believing the enemies' lies.

Every one of us would like to have the one spiritual experience that would make us a mature believer, able to resist any temptation that might come our way. Unfortunately, that is not possible. Rather, Paul says we are "transformed by the renewing of [our] mind" (Romans 12:2), and that takes time.

Weapon #3: *The Spirit of Christ*

"But I say, walk by the Spirit, and you will not carry out the desire of the flesh" (Galatians 5:16). When Christ ascended into heaven He poured out the gift of the Holy Spirit upon His Church. All believers are indwelt with the Spirit, but not all are filled with the Spirit—not all participate in the benefits of the Spirit's power. These are ours through cleansing, meditation and, above all, faith. As we receive Christ as Savior, so we must walk in Him.

ACTION STEP:
Submit yourself fully to the Holy Spirit and ask Him to give you the spiritual energy you need. Ask in faith, expecting to experience the fruit of the Spirit's work.

Weapon #4: *The Peace of Christ*

Visualize again the ancient medieval fort with guards standing at the high towers on the outside wall. Their responsibility is to watch for intruders and, if necessary, kill any enemies attempting to gain entrance.

This exact imagery is found in Scripture:

And let the peace of Christ rule in your hearts, to which indeed you were called in one body; and be thankful (Colossians 3:15).

The Greek word *brabeuo* translated "rule" is used only here in the New Testament and means "to act as an umpire." The idea is that peace should do the administering, ruling or deciding in our lives. One scholar defines it as "that calm of mind which is not ruffled by adversity, overclouded by sin or a remorseful conscience, or disturbed by fear and the approach of death."

We could paraphrase it: "Let the peace of Christ guard the entrance of your minds, refusing to admit any sin that would disturb that peace." The peace of Christ calls all the shots!

Look back on your experiences and I think you will agree that we fall into temptation when our mind is restless, distracted or prone to anxiety. When we do not experience the peace of Christ, our guard is down and rebel forces attempt to take control of the fortress.

ACTION STEP:
Frisk every thought that comes into your mind to make sure you are not allowing an enemy to come in. Paul lists characteristics of the thoughts that should be allowed entry: *"Whatever is true . . . honorable . . . right . . . pure . . . lovely . . . of good repute . . . any excellence . . . worthy of praise"* (Philippians 4:8).

Like a metal detector at an airport, we must be sensitized to thoughts that want to sneak past the peace of Christ standing guard over our heart. If that seems like a tall order, ask God to enable you to do it.

Weapon #5: *The People of Christ*

We will never be free of some of our thought patterns until we enlist the help of other believers. One of the most important weapons against Satan and his emissaries is humility. Humility before God always results in humility before others. When we confess our faults one to another, our enemies cringe. Pride is, after all, the one obsession that gives permission for all the others to survive in our souls.

Paul said, "We are destroying speculations" (2 Corinthians 10:5). That can be done by humble confession and soliciting the prayers of others in our battles against our enemies. The rooms of the castle must be made clean.

The needed surge of spiritual power normally can come only from other believers who covenant together to uphold one another before God in the spiritual battles of life.

A man who was unable to overcome his battle with pornography told me that when he confessed this sin to several other men who agreed to pray for him, God took it out of his life completely.

ACTION STEP:
Pray that God will lead you to a prayer partner. Begin meeting each week, sharing your personal needs — and expect results!

How long will it take for your mind to begin conforming to God's thoughts? That depends. If you are faithful in the steps listed here, you will begin to see results in two weeks. If you make them regular habits, you will find that transformation indeed is taking place. Someday you will look back and wonder why you ever found some of those sins so attractive. God will make the change through His Word.

Watch over your heart with all diligence,
For from it flow the springs of life (Proverbs 4:23).

4

FATAL ADDICTIONS

From blinding self-absorption to emotional and spiritual strength

"RICHARD BRZECZEK MADE IT to the top very fast," wrote Cheryl Lavin in the *Chicago Tribune,* but "he made it to the bottom even faster."[1]

Brzeczek, who was the superintendent of the Chicago Police Department, blew it all in four short years. By the time he was 42 he had been in and out of two psychiatric hospitals, had been humiliated in a run for Cook County State's Attorney, and had become an alcoholic and a victim of deep depression. To add to his guilt and misery, he had two affairs and was, in his words, "addicted to adultery."

There is a new term we are hearing much about these days; it's called "sexual addiction." This is the recognition that it is possible to become so powerless against sexual temptation that the victim gives in to it repeatedly, despite the guilt, depression and deceit accompanying such actions.

In Proverbs we read about the person who is like a city without walls. Quite literally he has no defenses; he succumbs to temptation without a fight—or if he does fight, he always loses.

In his book, *Addicted to Adultery: How We Saved Our Marriage / How You Can Save Yours,*[2] he and his wife tell the story of how affairs begin and how they end. They also give insight into the nature of sexual addiction.

Brzeczek's first affair began innocently enough. A flight attendant sat next to him during a trip to Washington. "From the moment she sat down next to me, there were certain silent messages between us . . . an electricity . . . a physical enticement that was new, exciting and very stimulating."

Though he loved his wife and was not looking for an affair, he and this woman, whom he calls Diane, shared some lunches and then a hotel room. The affair turned into an obsession. "It was like a fix," he says now. "For me to make a phone call to her was the equivalent of a junkie shooting up some heroin. If I didn't make the contact, I'd be hysterical. It was like withdrawal. I would be crying, sobbing uncontrollably."

Along with his obsession with Diane, he also became hooked on danger. He knew he could be caught, yet he took risks. He even found lying addictive. When he was deceptive the adrenalin would rush through him as he fabricated more stories and took even greater risks. He began a second affair and enjoyed the euphoria of seeing each woman without the other knowing.

When confronted with the evidence, he lied to his wife, a marriage counselor and his therapist. "I actually had the doctors convinced that I wasn't the one with the problem, but Liz was." In retrospect he wonders how he kept all of the lies straight while he was lying to three different women. "The stress of trying to remember what I told to whom was about to kill me. I'm surprised I didn't have a heart attack."

He began to drink more heavily, and this increased his guilt and depression. After he finally told his wife about the affairs, he promised to end the relationships. Yet that same day he promised Diane he would marry her. During his political campaign he would often have to cancel meetings because he was either intoxicated or depressed. The pressure was turned up a notch when he discovered he was being investigated for dipping into the police contingency fund. Little wonder he lost the race for State's Attorney to his opponent, Richard Daly.

Despite his intention to reform, the lying continued. He lied to his wife, children and friends. Of course he lied to himself too. Deviously manipulating so many people and seeing what all this was doing to his family made it almost impossible for him to look at himself in the mirror when he shaved in the morning.

During the next several months he lost all control over his life. He stopped shaving and showering and changing his clothes. He would phone his girlfriend in front of his wife and kids, begging her to come and be with him. He felt paralyzed and depressed. He would lie around and drink — and cry. He contemplated suicide.

Richard Brzeczek says he found God in the psychiatric ward where he stayed for more than a month. He credits God and his psychiatrist for the strength to break up with Diane. That was the beginning of the healing process. His marriage was saved despite the fact that on the day of his release he was indicted on 24 counts of theft and official misconduct. He was later acquitted of the charges.

The Brzeczeks have worked through their pain and are doing well, and now they are trying to help other couples save their marriages. The book is an honest account of the power of an adulterous relationship. Yes, there is such a thing as addiction to adultery.

THE SOURCE AND POWER
OF ADDICTION

Addiction. The word refers to compulsive behaviors that could control any of us. We all know about the power of alcohol, drugs and gambling, but today we also hear about workaholics and sex addicts. Some people are addicted to pornography or gambling, others to overeating.

Although addicts have existed since the beginning of the human race, it now appears that the number of people involved in destructive behavior is on the increase. The availability of drugs and pornography and the legalization of gambling all contribute to this escalation of addictive behavior.

More important, the breakup of the family provides the soil in which addictions can grow quickly. Powerful compulsions often can be traced to a dysfunctional family history—indeed addictions have been in some family lines for generations. In *Out of the Shadows: Understanding Sexual Addiction,* Patrick Carnes writes: "Sexual compulsiveness, like all addictions, rests in a complex web of family relationships."[3]

There are at least two ways of viewing addiction: as a disease or as sin. Some groups have labeled addiction a disease, hoping this will make it easier for the sufferer to seek help. There is no reason to be ashamed of having measles or a gallstone; neither is there any shame in having the disease of alcoholism or sexual compulsiveness.

The down side to this approach is, it makes the cure more difficult since the addict believes he bears no responsibility for catching the "disease."

Let us be honest and admit that addiction is nothing more than what Keith Miller has rightly stated it to be: the "blinding self-absorption called sin." He continues, "Sin is the universal addiction to self that develops when individuals put themselves in the center of their personal world in a way that leads to abuse of others or self. Sin causes sinners to seek instant gratification, to be first, and to get more than their share—now." In light of this, it is important for the addict to realize that

Christ has not promised to heal all of our diseases,
but He has promised to deliver us from our sins.

God has promised always to come to the aid of sinners who seek His forgiveness and help.

In the following pages I shall answer, from a biblical perspective, several common questions about addiction:

- What are the steps that lead to addiction?

- What are the chains that hold a person bound?

- And, finally, are there some keys—some principles—that can break the vicious cycle?

STEPS THAT LEAD TO ADDICTION

In Romans 1 Paul gives a spiritual history of the human race. Specifically, he discusses the origin of homosexuality. However, **first,** we must realize that *Paul is speaking here about the human race in general, not just the experience of the homosexual.* Because homosexuality is usually caused by environmental factors or molestation in childhood, a person who ends up in homosexuality may be totally unaware of the process Paul outlines here.

Second, the *steps listed here are applicable to all other sins and addictions as well.* Proof that we should give his words a wider interpretation is given in verses 28-32 where he lists a total of twenty-two sins that grow out of the spiritual decline of the human race.

Read this descending staircase that bottoms out in the wasteland of addiction, violence and perversion:

> For even though they knew God, they did not honor Him as God, or give thanks; but they became futile in their speculations, and their foolish heart was darkened. Professing themselves to be wise, they became fools, and exchanged the glory of the incorruptible God for an image in the form of corruptible man and of birds and four-footed animals and crawling creatures. Therefore God gave them over . . . (Romans 1:21-23).

They began by dishonoring God through failing even to recognize the creature/creator distinction, which often includes anger toward God and a callous disregard for His authority. This leads to hard-heartedness and a determination to tune God out of one's life and existence. What happened when God was not given His rightful place?

Step #1: *The true God was replaced with a false god.*

We are spiritual creatures, so we cannot live in a spiritual vacuum. For a man to live without a god is like asking a fish to live without water. Therefore when the true God is abandoned, another will be substituted. Just name an addict's addiction and you have named his god.

Step #2: *The truth of God was changed into a lie.*

God created us in such a way that it is difficult for us to violate what we know to be true. So in the interest of fulfilling our desires, we are prone to rationalize our behavior. The only way this can be done is to call God's truth a lie.

All addicts change the truth of God into a lie. Alcoholics and adulterers lie to other people, but what is more serious, they lie to themselves. They either tell themselves there is nothing wrong with their behavior or they blame others for what they are doing. Or they assure themselves that they are in full control of their particular vice, they are not addicted, and they can stop whenever they like. Besides, they have every right to live as they do.

This explains why addictions involve so much denial — nobody can practice destructive behavior without exchanging truth for lies. Truth and wholesome behavior are inseparably linked. When God's restraints are thrown off, truth must also be jettisoned.

Step #3: *The God-given natural functions were exchanged for unnatural ones.*

We all have basic needs that cry for fulfillment. When we leave God out, we tell ourselves we have every right to meet our needs without reference to God.

Addiction is nothing more than trying to meet legitimate needs in illegitimate ways. When a man squeezes God out of his thoughts, he ends up making many vain attempts to deaden the pain of an empty life. The result is a long list of sins which can become the root of any addiction (verses 28-32). We should not be surprised at multiple addictions — people running from one compulsion to another or involved with several at the same time. Addiction is a crutch, man's substitute for God's prescription for our fulfillment.

Most of the human race suffers from some kind of addiction. To be free from sin's power is the exception rather than the rule. You do not have to have a perverse streak of evil to become an addict. Addicts are normal people, people you work with, people you go to church with, people you live with. An addict can be anyone taking the path of least resistance, pursuing his innate desires with abandon. In fact, since the fall of man into sin, addiction is the natural state of mankind.

Addiction is a continuum, not a hardened absolute state. Some addicts are under the power of sin more than others, but all are fellow members of the human race. A consummate addict is one who has taken a few more wrong turns than his neighbor — assuming his neighbor isn't a consummate addict too.

Think of your life as a car with you at the wheel. An addict is simply someone who has lost control. His compulsive behaviors drive him as if his hand were no longer on the steering wheel.

In a previous chapter I referred to Ted Bundy, the criminal who confessed to killing 28 girls. He began reading pornography at a young age. As the excitement of seeing this material wore off, he sought to recreate the same euphoria he originally had experienced. He imagined what it would be like to molest a child, then he had to act it out to see if the experience was as great as he imagined it to be. Then he visualized strangling a child, to see if this would give him an even greater erotic experience.

After he did it the first time, he says, he could hardly believe he was capable of such an awful crime. Nevertheless, he craved to reach the same euphoric experience again and again—so the murders continued. He became a consummate addict.

You say, "Yes, but not all those who become addicted to pornography become child molesters or murderers." That is true; only a small percentage go on to those kinds of crimes. My point is that once you relinquish the control of your life to an addiction, once the steering wheel is out of your hands, it is no longer you who decides where the car will go. Not everyone who loses control lands in the same place. Some drive into a ditch and have a few bruises; others tumble into a valley and are permanently wounded; still others hit an on-coming car and innocent people are maimed or killed. When your life is out of control, *where you eventually land is no longer for you to decide.* That decision is made by forces beyond you.

To continue the car analogy, every so often an addict experiences a "near miss." The homosexual thinks he has contracted AIDS, the alcoholic is fired from his job, and the adulterer fears his wife will discover his affair. The child molester is terrified he might have been seen, and the gambler is tossed out of his apartment because he blew all his money. These people swear they will quit their destructive behavior, and many of them do — for a time.

Successful as these interludes may be, they only give an illusion of control. Usually, they are only preludes to a more daring adventure in the future. Soon the addict is back to the guilt-ridden cycle. I'm reminded of Mark Twain's cryptic remark, "Of course I can quit smoking. I've done it a thousand times!"

Why is their reform short-lived? They have not been willing to face the pain of self-evaluation or the issues they will have to deal with in reestablishing contact with God. Addicts have been known to lie, cheat, manipulate, shift blame, steal, and make others feel guilty for their problems. They do this because they do not want to face the secret chains that hold them bound to their sin.

CHAINS THAT KEEP ADDICTS BOUND

Why is it so hard to walk away from an addiction? Why not just wake up some morning and say, "Enough is enough!" and leave it all behind?

Powerful, secret chains will not let the addict be free. Those chains are much stronger than he is, and after a while he refuses to contest their power.

What are those secret chains?

Chain #1: *Guilt and shame*

The addict is constantly violating his own moral standards. He knows that what he is doing contradicts his upbringing and standards of decency. He also knows that he is hurting himself and others, but he continues the difficult task of a double existence — one life in his family and society, the other in his world of addiction.

Even more threatening is the fact that he knows God sees his every move. His hypocrisy tears at him, for he knows all too well that he is but a human shell.

In his mind he cannot afford to be honest, for then the game would be over. He must lie to others and to himself. The guilt and shame become excruciating; he sees no way out. He continues to be torn apart, a part of him wanting to be free, another part believing life without his addiction would be unbearable.

Chain #2: *Dishonesty*

Fear of exposure is so painful that even when he is discovered he evades the truth. The smart addict has readied himself for just such a moment. He has spent hours arming himself with a whole pack of lies he can use at any moment. Since the addict's whole life is a lie, telling one more is of no great moral significance.

The more he lies the greater his guilt and shame. Increasingly, telling the truth is more difficult. Even when he decides to "come clean" he usually will tell only part of the story. Dishonesty is another of his many crutches.

Chain #3: *Euphoria*

No one can calculate the number of hours the addict spends trying to work out schemes that will give him the euphoria he seeks without being discovered. Just the plans themselves bring a rush of excitement.

The addict thinks no one else has ever experienced the intensity of pleasure he receives through his addiction. No one, he thinks, can understand the elation and satisfaction that can come from pornography, alcoholism or drugs. If he is addicted to gambling, he is driven by the euphoria of taking a risk, of making a bet. No one, he thinks, can understand his impassioned sensations.

The addict thinks he cannot live without this experience of pleasure. All of his psychic energy is spent trying to figure out how to make sure nothing will ever come between him and his beautiful feeling. The alcoholic, for example, is obsessed with making sure he will always have his precious bottle, no matter what.

The voyeur is consumed with the rush of pleasure that comes when he sees a partially clad woman through a bedroom window. Just the anticipation gives him erotic excitement. He will spend hours in the dark waiting for those 20 seconds of nudity. He becomes a slave to the waves of sensation that pulse through his body.

The tycoon on Wall Street who already has a hundred million dollars but cheats to get more is addicted to "the deal." That is his shot of heroin. He is quite literally addicted to greed. Wielding power over other people becomes his fix.

Adultery, gambling, overeating — all of these can become a titillating obsession. These feelings of euphoria become the sole motive for the addict's existence. He is terrified of being unable to experience these special feelings over and over again.

This ought to be a warning to all of us, a warning never to become involved in addictive behavior. Those first steps may create within us sensations that we will want repeated over and over again. It is better never to have experienced the exhilaration of alcohol, drugs, pornography or adultery. We could become a slave to the euphoria, a slave to those waves of pleasure that surge through the human body.

Chain #4: *Fear of rejection*

The addict might want to go to someone for help, but he cannot bear to do so for fear he would be rejected, despised and thought a sick pervert. Yet above all, he has the emotional need to be accepted as a person with value and with the potential for a better life.

So he is between a rock and a hard place. If he tells his story, he will be rejected. Yet the only way for him to get out of his prison is to be able to share the whole story with a fellow human being and still be loved and accepted.

Have you ever wondered why Alcoholics Anonymous is successful? One of the most powerful forces for transformation is honest interaction with other people who are fighting the same battles. That's why we have so many other anonymous groups today — sex addicts, gamblers, overeaters, etc. The addict says, "Finally I've found someone who understands my struggle, and he can't reject me, because he's in the same predicament I am!"

Possibly these groups had to begin outside the established church because too many people felt they could never be honest about their addictions in a church atmosphere where no one will admit to having such problems. Thankfully, that is changing as many churches are beginning special ministries to addicts of various kinds.

Chain #5: *Loneliness*

Loneliness? Perhaps a distraught wife says, "No, that can't be true of an addict. My husband was an alcoholic and he wasn't lonely at all. In fact, I bore him ten children."

Many people who are surrounded by others are lonely, though. They feel no one really understands them, and worse, if anyone did, they would reject them.

Addicts usually end up withdrawing from society, satisfied with only the minimal interaction needed to function. Eventually, they also withdraw from their families.

In order to cope with all the internal pain, they often resort to violent behavior. An addict of any type may abuse his wife, beat his children, and display many other forms of irrational hostility. Meanwhile he shifts the blame for his behavior to others, because he cannot bear to admit the truth.

Chain #6: *Sense of Worthlessness*

Addictions often develop as a result of the pain caused by dysfunctional family relationships. Sometimes the roots of addiction even span generations.

If you were abused, you will have a greater propensity to escape from your pain in self-defeating, compulsive, addictive behavior. If you were thrown onto the street at a young age, you will have a much stronger tendency to deaden the pain by seeking the cheap thrills of pornography, alcoholism, drugs, etc. Eventually these will become the crutches you will convince yourself you need in order to cope with reality. The addictions become your god—you believe only they can get you from point *A* to point *B*.

Working through the question of self-identity is painful, and that is one more reason so many people prefer to continue in their addiction rather than to change their behavior. Change is feared, for it means that the addict has to come to terms with himself.

Call it what you will, addicts live in an emotional vacuum. They have deep needs they are trying to meet. Unfortunately they do this in ways that will leave them with even deeper needs. Like men drifting helplessly in a boat on a saltwater sea, the more they drink to slake their thirst, the more thirsty they become.

The alcoholic drinks to overcome the problems caused by his alcoholism, and the sex addict opts for a series of sexual encounters to hide the pain caused by his immorality. The gambler makes bets to try to cover the losses incurred by his gambling. Little wonder the addict hates himself and does all he can to insulate himself from reality.

KEYS TO UNLOCK THE PRISONS

Addictions are not new. They have been around since the fall of man in Eden.

The church in Corinth was trying to survive in a culture inundated with immoral addictions. Just up the hill was a temple dedicated to prostitution. One thousand free prostitutes were available for the populace. Every form of sexual sin was practiced without shame or inhibition.

Converts out of that culture brought with them the struggles we are so familiar with today. Some new believers wanted to legitimatize their behavior; they wanted to bend the rules so they could feel comfortable without giving up their cherished pleasures.

To these Paul wrote:

> Do you not know that the unrighteous shall not inherit the kingdom of God? Do not be deceived; neither fornicators, nor idolaters, nor adulterers, nor effeminate, nor homosexuals, nor thieves, nor the covetous, nor drunkards, nor revilers, nor swindlers, shall inherit the kingdom of God. And such were some of you; but you were washed, but you were sanctified, but you were justified in the name of the Lord Jesus Christ, and in the Spirit of our God (1 Corinthians 6:9-11).

Name your addiction, and Paul mentions it, at least in its root form. Yet he also says this was the *past experience* of believers and not their present disposition.

Those in spiritual slavery would not inherit the kingdom — that is, they would forfeit rule with Christ in the age to come. (The question of whether this means they would not be allowed entrance into the kingdom is debated by scholars.) One thing is certain: God regarded their sin as serious.

Paul uses three words to describe the keys, or principles, that free a person from the enslaving power of addictions. Those key words are *washed, sanctified, justified*. Scholars are puzzled as to why the sequence seems to be backwards — we would say justification is first. But Paul is simply beginning with the individual's experience and working back to the basis of it.

Key #1: *Washed — forgiven*

That means the guilt and shame that bound these believers is taken away.

Have you ever used a water hose to clean a gutter? Under pressure a stream of water can take all the dirt and pollution away. When God applies His cleansing, our conscience can be made clean.

Think of what this means to the addict—to have all the guilt and shame washed away! No longer a voice of condemnation, no longer the feelings of hypocrisy and self-incrimination. Cleansed!

Sometimes we need others to confirm that we have been cleansed by God. We can be helped in the process by the instruction of pastors and teachers who have been given to the church. Yes, God has forgiven us, but the body of Christ can help make that a reality to us.

Key #2: *Sanctified—set apart*

The word *sanctified* has the same root as the word *holy*. This means that we are special to God—we are not ordinary, but extraordinary. I know an artist who is so in love with a particular picture that he built a special wall for it in his new home. If that picture were a person, he would know he is very special to his owner.

We have been set apart by God for special treatment. The person who comes to Christ, regardless of his past, is assured a place of prominence. Yes, there is a purpose for living; yes, God is not finished with us yet.

Key #3: *Justified—accepted*

Despite their past behavior, God declared the believers in Corinth to be as righteous as Christ. That's what justification means.

Every person justified by God receives the same righteousness, without distinction. The homosexual, alcoholic and adulterer all have the same acceptance and privileges before God as the person who has escaped all these addictions.

Think of what this means to the addict—he can be number one on God's list of things to take care of in the universe! This is the beginning of freedom from the chains that bind. Receiving the gift of eternal life through Christ is the doorway, the first step in the walk to freedom. You must begin by knowing that you belong to God, that you have been cleansed by Him. The shackles of guilt and shame must be broken.

The first step listed by Alcoholics Anonymous is the humble acknowledgment that you cannot fight this battle on your own. The "Higher Power" that can lead you to freedom is the God and Father of our Lord Jesus Christ.

REASONS TO STAY FREE AND PURE

Is that the end of the struggle? No, because you need to work through the internal struggles that led you into the addiction in the first place. There may be many battles. This is when the body of Christ needs to step in, help fill the emotional vacuum, and provide support and encouragement to the addict in his battle for a pure life.

Paul gives three reasons believers should live sexually pure. These reasons are based upon the fact that the entire Trinity – Father, Son and Holy Spirit – stand by to help us in our need. God becomes our ally in the fight for moral purity.

Reason #1: *We are joined to Christ*

Do you not know that your bodies are members of Christ? (1 Corinthians 6:15).

That fact gives us the right to break all obligations to our addiction. Our bond to Christ is stronger than our bond to destructive behavior. What this means will become clearer in the next chapter.

Here is a point of elementary knowledge: If you are a part of Christ, and I am a part of Christ, then we are joined to each other. If God has washed, sanctified and justified you, who am I to reject you?

The only form in which Christ's body exists on earth is in His people. Look through the Gospels and you will find that Christ was constantly welcoming desperate sinners into His presence.

Reason #2: *We are indwelt by the Holy Spirit*

Do you not know that your body is a temple of the Holy Spirit who is in you, whom you have from God, and that you are not your own? (1 Corinthian 6:19)

In the old Testament there were two parts to the Temple, the outer court (the Temple area) and the inner shrine where God dwelt (the Holy of Holies). The Greek word Paul uses here is *naos*, which means the "inner shrine." In practical terms, this means that the Holy of Holies has been transferred to our human bodies. God dwells within us.

Therefore, the addict has the possibility of emotional healing. That "hole in the soul" that fuels the addiction can be filled with wholeness. The loneliness, guilt and shame can be replaced by what the Holy Spirit is committed to do in our lives, namely to bring about needed emotional and spiritual strength.

The work of the Spirit is so wholesome, so fulfilling that it is more than an adequate substitute for the euphoria created by the addictions we have talked about. It is peace without guilt and love without bitterness. That's why Paul says, "Do not get drunk with wine, for that is dissipation, but be filled with the Spirit" (Ephesians 5:18).

Reason #3: *We belong to God*

For you have been bought with a price: therefore glorify God in your body (1 Corinthians 6:20).

Here we have the answer to our sense of worthlessness. The God of the universe purchased us at high cost. We belong to His family. Whatever our background, whatever hurts have been created by our human family, God can heal them by giving us a new identity in His family.

I do not want to hold out the promise that your addictions will immediately disappear, though I do know of some people who were delivered instantly by Christ. More realistically, I believe the inner work of God in the soul is so sure and so steady that eventually the addiction drops away like dead leaves from a tree in the fall.

GROWING WITHIN

If you have an addiction, I can tell you with certainty that you are not emotionally whole. If you walked into my room with a crutch, I would know you have a physical ailment. If you have an addiction, it is just as sure a sign that you have a spiritual and emotional hurt that needs attention. As God does the healing within, the crutch gets thrown away.

You cannot give up your addiction on your own — but you can come to Christ with God's help. You can be washed, sanctified and justified.

I'm not asking you to give up your behavior cold turkey. If you come to Christ *as you are* and receive Him, He is able to bring about the healing you need. When your secrets are finally exposed to God and to others who can help you, recovery becomes a possibility.

You come as you are but you leave as a new person — and the transformation begins. Like the crutches, your addiction becomes obsolete as God, through His presence, His power, and His people, brings wholeness to your soul.

Thousands can say there *is* life after addiction.

5

THE HURT AND HEALING OF ABUSE

Four ways Jesus heals the broken-hearted

Feel the pain of the woman who wrote this letter to Ann Landers:

My father, an alcoholic, began to abuse me when I was five years old. I finally found the courage to tell my mother five years later. She called me a liar and a troublemaker. After several weeks of my pleading and crying, throwing up and having nightmares, she said, "I will leave it up to you. I will go to the police if you want me to, but they will put your father in jail and we will all probably starve to death."

Being an insecure, emotionally troubled 10-year-old, I could not face that burden, so I chose to let the abuse go on. A year later my father stopped abusing me and began to abuse my 5- and 7-year-old cousins who were living with us at the time.

He died when I was 28. I did not cry at his funeral. My mother died nine years later, and I cried hysterically at hers — and every day after that for several weeks.

I went for counseling and learned that I forgave my father because I came to understand that he was a sick man, but I could not forgive my mother because she didn't protect me against him.

My relationships with men have been awful. My drug of choice was food. I am now in a 12-step program and getting better. Ann, please keep telling people who have been abused that silence is deadly. They **must** *talk about it and get it out in the open. Only then will the healing begin.*

P. J. in West Hartford

Nothing is more deserving of tears than the plight of children in our society. Who can begin to count the buckets of tears that have been shed by children (and adults) who have been abused by those who should have loved them the most?

Thousands of adults languish in emotional distress, unable to make peace with the trauma of their childhood. To put such a past behind them is difficult; thankfully, it is not impossible.

Abuse can take different forms. One is **verbal abuse**. Some parents call their child names, predict future failure and severely criticize him (or her). Let's not think this abuse is not painful. There are thousands of people who can scarcely function because of destructive words lodged like arrows in their souls.

A well-known singer whose father berated her as a child even now cannot seem to overcome the emotional roadblocks erected by those harsh, uncaring words. To quote her, "Though a thousand people tell me I sing well, I cannot believe them, for the little girl in me still asks, 'If they are speaking the truth, why did my daddy tell his little girl she couldn't sing? Why would Daddy say how awful she was?' Something inside me says my daddy could not be wrong."

Though that daddy has been dead since 1984, this woman says, "I want to be emotionally whole, but my daddy stands in the way." The power of verbal abuse.

Add to this the ugly reality of **physical abuse**. I do not dare tell the stories that appear almost daily in the newspapers: stories of children locked in closets, beaten mercilessly, tied to bedposts, drowned in bathtubs. If just speaking of these atrocities causes us pain, imagine what it is like for the children who actually endure them.

Sexual abuse is rampant throughout the land. A father molests his daughters; brothers and sisters are involved in various levels of experimentation. And what happens in some schools and day-care centers? And what have some baby-sitters done?

Incredibly, one out of every four baby girls born this year eventually will be sexually molested by somebody, likely a member of her family, a relative or a trusted friend. In fact, sexual abuse occurs in all kinds of homes, Christian and non-Christian, rich and poor, educated and non-educated.

How many abusers are there in the world? We don't know, of course, but some have molested hundreds of children. Others just one or two. We do know their numbers are increasing.

SPECIAL PROBLEMS OF THE ABUSED

What are the special problems experienced by those who suffer such childhood trauma?

Intense Anger

Take a walk in the sandals of those who have been abused. Yes, they may be adults now, but part of their life is missing. Somebody has stolen their happiness. It's not just because they remember the pain of the past, but it is also that the emotional paralysis does not allow them to function in the present.

Thanks to the abusers, these victims may now be unable to love, to trust or to relate with others in freedom. They also may fail repeatedly in their activities, believing they are programmed for defeat.

What makes matters worse, their abuser likely got away with it; he is unpunished and totally unconcerned about the pain he inflicted. He may simply go from victim to victim without a twinge of conscience. Understandably, his victims are filled with resentment.

These victims also may be angry with God. When I urged one woman to deal with the abuse she suffered, she asked the troubling question referred to earlier in this book, "If God wasn't there for me when I was being abused, why should I think He would be there for me now? *I can never trust Him.*"

Victims of abuse are often angry—very angry. This may result in depression and anxiety.

Don't be quick to judge them. How would you feel if someone you trusted stole your childhood? Anger is understandable.

The Bondage of Shame

Children have an innate respect for those two people who gave them life. They not only think that father and mother can do no wrong, but they crave the acceptance and love of their parents. When a parent abuses a child, the child believes he is getting his just deserts. To his way of thinking he is just as bad as his parents have made him out to be. Justice, children believe, is being served.

This explains why a woman who has been abused by her father will seek to marry a man who will continue to abuse her. What she is saying in effect is, "I deserve to be abused, so I need to find someone who will give me what I deserve."

About 75 percent of parents who abuse their children were themselves abused as children. There is a bonding to abuse.

A child who has been sexually abused feels dirty, unworthy and ashamed. One abused woman said she felt as if she had "Damaged Goods" written on her forehead. No one, she thought, could possibly love her.

Such a woman may follow through with what is called the "abused woman syndrome," seeking immoral relationships and even prostitution. Others become passive victims looking for someone to abuse them. They live out the dark stain that smudges their soul. Some, thankfully, become emotionally whole.

Abusers have a way of making their captors feel guilty. A father may lead his daughter to believe she is a co-conspirator, an accomplice in what happened. And of course, since we are sexual creatures, a child may eventually enjoy the sexual sensations of the abuse. All of this combines to compound the guilt.

Difficulty in Establishing Deep Relationships.

Those who have been abused find it difficult to trust others—they become fearful if a relationship becomes too personal and intimate. It is very common for victims to sabotage the very relationships they so desperately need. Those who have been rejected tend to act in such a way as to insure more rejection.

The abused often have two unconscious agendas. **First**, they feel the need to *prove that no one is trustworthy*. Having been betrayed by the person who should have protected them, they are convinced that all men (or women) are the same. Thus they will become critical and suspicious, attitudes symptomatic of their distrust.

Second, they will try to *prove that no one can love them*. After all, they perceive themselves unworthy of love, and they believe that all love is conditional. It is not uncommon for them to test every relationship to the limit, to make impossible demands from those who befriend them, insisting that someone else is responsible to make them happy. When their friends pull away from the relationship, they feel they have proven their point, and they exclaim, "See? Nobody really loves me!"

In a marriage relationship, the problem becomes excruciating. The formerly abused partner is impossible to please. By becoming critical, angry and clinging to unreasonable expectations, the victim inevitably makes life impossible. Intimacy becomes a threat to the abused partner who does not feel loved but "used." Because a close relationship has been made nigh impossible, the marriage is soon in deep trouble.

As David Seamands wrote in *The Healing of Memories*, "When painful memories have not been faced, healed and integrated into life, they often break through defenses and interfere with normal living."[1]

Those of us who were not abused must be patient with these victims. Our greatest contribution is to assure them of our love and acceptance, no matter what story they tell us about their past. On the other hand, we also must be aware of the games that are being played; we must not allow them to manipulate us with guilt. Sometimes there has to be loving but firm confrontation.

Most important, we can give them hope. We can assure them that there is life after abuse. Thousands have changed their status from *victim* to *survivor*.

If this sounds impossible to you, remember that it is exactly what Christ offers—a life that is supernatural. Resources are available for this transformation.

CHRIST, THE HEALER OF BROKEN HEARTS

What, specifically, can Christ do for those who hurt? One day Christ went into a temple in Nazareth and took down a scroll, turned to a few paragraphs in Isaiah and read them. When He was finished He said, "Today this Scripture is fulfilled in your hearing" (Luke 4:21).

This passage speaks of Christ's ability to deliver His people from captivity, the power He uses to free prisoners. It speaks of Christ as the physician of the soul. The Isaiah passage reads:

> The Spirit of the Lord GOD is upon me,
> Because the LORD has anointed me
> To bring good news to the afflicted;
> He has sent me to bind up the brokenhearted,
> To proclaim liberty to captives,
> And freedom to prisoners;
> To proclaim the favorable year of the LORD,
> And the day of vengeance of our God;
> To comfort all who mourn,
> To grant those who mourn in Zion,
> Giving them a garland instead of ashes,
> The oil of gladness instead of mourning,
> The mantle of praise instead of a spirit of fainting.
> So they will be called oaks of righteousness,
> The planting of the LORD, that He may be glorified.
>   (Isaiah 61:1-3)

The Jews had been hauled off to Babylon by the thousands because of their persistent idolatry. There they wept, longing for the day when they could return to Jerusalem. Here the prophet writes about Christ who would eventually deliver them. The context refers to literal, political fulfillment.

Yet Christ's use of this prophecy in Luke 4 gives us permission to apply the passage spiritually. He came to release us from any prison that will keep us from spiritual freedom.

He has been anointed to bring good news to the afflicted and to "bind up the brokenhearted." We usually think of binding up a broken arm, not a broken heart, but just as setting a broken bone helps it heal correctly, so Christ sets a broken heart so it will heal to the best of its ability. The heart still will have a scar, but spiritually speaking it will be functional; it will not have a gaping wound. Healing will have taken place.

How does Christ do this for His people?

He Frees You From Your Captor

If you have abuse in your background, ask yourself who still holds you bound. Your captor is anyone who has destructive authority over you. Christ came to set us free from those spiritual and emotional prisons others have built for us. He came to open the gates of the cell so we can walk out.

Here are some examples of captors whose power Christ can break:

(1) Your abuser

Who is the person who stole your childhood, who callously refused to hear your sobs and who betrayed your trust? Christ can break his authority over you.

Unfortunately, many people need to be free from the destructive influence of their parents. God put it within the heart of every child to desire a father and mother who love him. Parents are to protect him and give him the security he needs as a child in order to grow up and become a responsible adult. The deepest hurt a child can have is not the death of a father or mother, but the betrayal of one or both of them. The verbal, physical and sexual abuse from a parent who should protect a child brings a raw wound of sorrow and pain.

Recently, I spoke to a man who is so emotionally numb that he lives without feelings. He was raised by an irrational, paranoid mother who abused him physically and verbally. She called him names. She told him he would always be a failure just like his father. She hated all men in general and her husband in particular, and she vented this hatred upon her son. He told me, "You must understand that for me to succeed in my mother's eyes is to fail, for the only dream she ever had for me was failure. To this day, I can still hear her curses in my ears."

I was moved to put my hand on his shoulder and pray for him, trusting God to break all the negative influence his mother ever had on him. Slowly he is being led out of his prison built by an apparently uncaring woman whom he called "Mother."

Yes, we must honor our father and mother, but no child should be bound by his parents' madness. We esteem their position, but there are times when we must respectfully smash all of their misused authority in our lives. The influence of abusive parents must be broken whether they are dead or alive.

(2) Your sexual partner, past or present

One day I spoke to a sixteen-year-old girl who had been seduced by an older married man. When the affair was discovered he blamed it all on her, as if he were to be exonerated. She was filled with anger and shame. Yet interestingly, she said to me, "Despite the hurt of being betrayed, if I met him on the street today and he asked me to go with him, even marry him, I would."

Such stories are legion. One fine Christian girl refused to respond to the overtures of an older, immoral man. One day in exasperation, he raped her. Despite the humiliation and shame, the girl became his slave, willing to do whatever he asked. She actually became his voluntary prisoner.

Sexual intercourse is not merely the union of two bodies but also the union of two spirits. Indeed, even intercourse with a prostitute makes a man one flesh with her (1 Corinthians 6:16). This means total union, a uniting of souls and spirits, and it makes it impossible to walk away from that relationship easily—a "soul-tie" has been developed that brings about a powerful unity and the possible control of one person over another.

This does not mean that when two people have sex they are joined in marriage, for marriage necessitates a covenant. Nevertheless, sex does join two people in such a close union that some counselors have discovered that if one of the partners is demonized (that is, under the control of evil spirits) there can be transference of such spirits during intercourse. Whenever this happens the cruel control of one partner over the other becomes complete. Thus a man may not be able to give up an adulterous partner, regardless of the damage he does to himself or his family; or a woman may become the slave of a man.

The union of souls during intercourse explains why sexual relationships outside of marriage end so badly, with feelings of hatred and betrayal amid intermittent attempts at loyalty. Two people who have been joined into one are being torn apart.

A person who has had an immoral relationship must trust Christ to break the soul-tie that can keep that person imprisoned by his or her captor. Of course, breaking such a relationship is not always easy because the captor may be able to cash in on a number of "I.O.U.'s" such as the threat of exposure or other forms of blackmail.

Christ can enable those who find themselves in the tangled web of immoral relationships to be free. The chains of authority of tyrants who would hold others in their grasp can be broken.

(3) A cultist partner

The most terrifying slavery I have ever seen was a young woman I knew who came under the authority of a man with occult powers. He held her captive, forcing her to do different kinds of unnatural and violent acts. He threatened her with death if she were to leave him, assuring her that he would trace her and always discover her whereabouts. She was terrified and confused, not knowing where to turn. She could not stay away from this man for more than a few hours. She was literally his slave.

Many cultists brainwash their captives to where they will even die for the leader. These cultists bring the unwary into subjection to their authority through the guise of spiritual leadership. Why don't the prisoners just up and leave? We ask that question only because we do not understand the awesome power a satanically inspired person can have over others. We do not understand soul-ties.

If you want your heart to be healed, you must not be under the abusive authority of anyone who is evil, anyone who manipulates you or takes you captive. You are to be a slave only of Christ, not of your parents, nor of a friend who wants to control you. You are not to be subject to some real or imagined person who has the power to program your soul.

What if you are married to such a person? What if there is abuse going on in your home now? If that is the case, you have the responsibility to share that information with someone who can help you. You also must realize that Christ can bring you out from under such a destructive influence. If you are faithful, He will do it in His own time and in His own way.

There are thousands of borderline cases, though, where control and abuse are not well differentiated. A wife lives as best she can with an alcoholic husband and the children are mistreated only occasionally. Or a paranoid mother neglects her children or manipulates them with guilt. Abuse can take a thousand forms.

The negative effects of these influences must be broken; the soul must remain free even while the abuse is happening. Christ can protect His people from the harmful effects; He can preserve the soul.

There is a passage in *Uncle Tom's Cabin* where a slave was being beaten but "it was as if the blows fell only on his body, not his soul." God can protect your spirit from evil influences even if your body must still endure the verbal and physical blows of your abuser.

Christ Dispenses Justice

Perhaps the greatest obstacle to our emotional wholeness is bitterness, the resentment generated when we are mistreated. To see the guilty one—the one who ruined our lives—go free only increases the anger. The injustice of it all causes us to cry out, "Where is God?"

The Babylonians mistreated the Israelites when they captured them and took them from Jerusalem to Babylon about the year 586 B.C. That was about 2500 years ago. Our passage, Isaiah 61:1-3, predicts the Babylonians will fall under the vengeance of God. That has not yet happened.

Interestingly, when Christ read this passage in the synagogue, He stopped before he got to the phrase "and the day of vengeance of our God." Why? Because vengeance awaits the second coming; it was not to be a part of the first. So, even though the Babylonians were conquered by Cyrus in 539 B.C., they still have not yet been fully judged by God.

If the Israelites have waited for twenty-five centuries and have not yet seen God avenge them, we should not be surprised if we are asked to wait awhile for God to "even the score." Someday there will be a resurrection of all individuals who have ever lived. Each personal life will be reviewed in minute detail, day by day, hour by hour. At that time vengeance will be meted out in exact proportion to the sins committed.

What is the implication? It's this: If you have been abused, the responsibility of bringing your captor to trial does not rest with you. Of course we should do all we can to promote justice, and those who have committed crimes should be dealt with in the courts. However, man can do only so much. There are always loose ends and circumstances where justice has been circumvented. In this life many people escape the judgment due them, but eventually God will rule on every single act that has ever been committed by all individuals who have ever lived.

That's why you can forgive without surrendering justice. The sin (or perhaps the crime) that was committed against you will be paid for. The abuser either will find refuge in Christ who appeased God for sinners, or he will bear the weight of his sin forever in hell. Either way, your case will be brought before the Almighty and He will have the last word.

Has not your abuser done enough damage to you already? Must he continue to ruin your life by creating this lump of bitterness in your heart? You must, for your own benefit, let go of that bitterness and entrust your complaint wholly to God.

Should you ever confront your abuser? Sometimes it may be necessary, but as I already have pointed out, in about 80 percent of the cases the perpetrator will deny he (or she) did anything wrong (that's part of the denial referred to in a previous chapter). If he denies it, the correct response from you is, "You may deny it, but God and I both know you are guilty. I now transfer to you all responsibility for what happened." This response can be either verbal or an attitude of the heart, whichever is appropriate to the situation. In either case, having made it, leave it there.

You must choose to forgive, for bitterness is one of the chains that will hold you in its grasp.

The fact that God will vindicate the oppressed establishes their dignity. At last someone will defend them, take up their cause and stand in their place. What the parents of an abused child did not do, God will accomplish.

He will take up the cause of His children, for "The LORD supports the afflicted" (Psalm 147:6).

What else does Christ do for the broken-hearted?

He Comforts You.

You say, "Is there a way to make up for my past?" Not so far as time is concerned, because we can never go back and relive the years that have gone by. Nevertheless, God does pour His comfort into our souls. He *appoints* for us blessings to take away the burdens of the past. Here is what He says He will do for the Israelites:

*(1) He will give them a crown of beauty
instead of ashes (Isaiah 61:3, NIV).*

During times of mourning, the ancients often threw ashes on their head. God was about to give them a new headpiece.

Does the name *Amnon* mean anything to you? He was one of the sons of David, a half-brother to Absalom. Amnon fell in love with Tamar who was his half-sister. He wanted to have sexual intercourse with her, so he set a scheme into action. He pretended to be sick and requested that Tamar come into the room to prepare some food for him. When she did this he jumped up from the bed and asked her to have sex with him. She protested, so in anger he raped her. What do you think that did to the relationship? We read:

> Then Amnon hated her with a very great hatred; for the hatred with which he hated her was greater than the love with which he had loved her. And Amnon said to her, "Get up, go away!" (2 Samuel 13:15).

How do you think Tamar felt? She had resisted him, and now that he was finished with her, he treated her like dirt. She said, "No. Sending me away would be even more evil than having raped me." She didn't want to let him get away with this. What did Amnon do? He asked his attendant to throw the woman out and lock the door. For

the whole story, read 2 Samuel 13. It details her response
to the shame and humiliation:

> And Tamar put ashes on her head, and tore her long-
> sleeved garment which was on her [a symbol of her vir-
> ginity]; and she put her hand on her head and went away,
> crying aloud as she went (v. 19).

Here was a young woman, raped by an incestuous
half-brother, filled with shame and anger. How did she
express it? With ashes on her head. Ashes symbolized
shame and humiliation.

In the Isaiah passage God says He will take the
ashes away and replace them with a garland, an ornamen-
tal headdress that was used for times of rejoicing. The King
James Version translates it "beauty." Yes, the turban was
worn for festive occasions and was a symbol of prosperity
and victory.

You may have been sexually violated by a brother,
father or friend you trusted. Symbolically, you have ashes
on your head, but God makes you look beautiful. There is
hope after abuse.

*(2) He will give them the oil of gladness
instead of mourning.*

Perfumed ointment was poured on guests at joy-
ous feasts. When David wrote, "He anointed my head with
oil," he was speaking of the special treatment God gives
those whom He loves. It was a high honor to be anointed
with the soothing oil.

If you attended a funeral in ancient times, you
did not come with your head anointed with oil. Oil symbolized joy; it was inappropriate in times of grief. God says
Israel will be blessed with the oil of gladness. The funeral
will give way to the wedding.

*(3) He will give them garments of praise
     instead of a spirit of fainting.*

Your clothing will be bright and beautiful — not sackcloth that indicates despondency. David wrote:

> I would have despaired unless I had believed
>   that I would see the goodness of the LORD
> In the land of the living.
> Wait for the LORD;
> Be strong, and let your heart take courage;
> Yes, wait for the LORD (Psalm 27:13,14).

All three of these blessings God promised the Israelites are outer changes that signify inward healing. The new look *without* reflects the new joy *within*.

Conclusion:

> They will be called oaks of righteousness, the planting of the LORD, that He may be glorified (Isaiah 61:3*b).*

Just as God liberated the Israelites, so He is ready to help us walk in the light of His love and freedom.

Christ Vindicates the Captor

Christ stands ready to free the abused, but what about the abuser? He too can have forgiveness if he seeks it. I received an anonymous letter from a man who had abused a boy. He explained the torment he was now going through and said, "I would give anything if I could undo the damage I did to that child."

Yes, abusers are human too. They do terrible things because they also are victims, locked in their own prison of anger, shame and perversion. Only God knows the torment of their conscience, the contempt they have for themselves, and the dreadful secrets that hold them bound.

Christ offers Himself to all men if they come to Him in humility and faith. As David learned:

> For my father and my mother have forsaken me,
> But the LORD will take me up (Psalm 27:10).

STEPS TO FREEDOM

How do you get from under the burden of your abuser, the person who keeps you in an emotional prison? These steps are not necessarily consecutive; sometimes they are done in reverse order, sometimes simultaneously. They may have to be repeated many times.

Step #1: *Confront your past — with Christ*

Don't delve into your past alone. You need the help of Christ and also a trusted friend or friends as you admit what has happened.

I cannot tell you how much of your past you must relive in order to be emotionally healed. Some find that simply acknowledging the abuses of the past is all that is necessary. Others need to confront their past in more detail. I do not believe that everyone who has been abused needs extensive therapy. Many people spend years sifting through their past only to discover that their investigation has not freed them from its power. Sometimes the more details uncovered, the greater the resentment and anger.

For some people it is enough to know that Jesus Christ is aware of every detail of their past. There is no rule that fits everyone, but the following guidelines will help. As you take your tour through the painful experiences of life, remember:

a. You do not have to confront all of your past at once. Take a bit of it — one experience — and relive it in the presence of God, telling Him how you felt, expressing your hurt and anger. Choose to forgive, and give your feelings — yes, your deepest feelings — to God.

b. You must share your hurt with a trusted friend or counselor who will feel your pain and share your burden. You must experience the acceptance and love of a human being regardless of what you tell that person about your past. Shame, anger and resentment—your friend must accept all of these outbursts without rejecting you.

c. Your dignity must be restored by understanding who you are in the presence of God and in the eyes of others. This will come through the comfort of Christ and His ambassadors, your friend(s).

d. Some people find help in writing a letter to their abuser, sharing all their hurt and anger (even if the letter is never sent). Others pretend that he (or she) is in an empty chair and they speak what is on their mind. These methods may be helpful in getting your past and its hurts out into the open.

You will need courage to embark on this journey. Let me assure you of one fact: There is nothing you will uncover in your past that you and God cannot handle. Heaven can heal the sorrows of earth.

Step #2: *Commit your past—to Christ*

You may find there are many loose ends you can never resolve on earth. Your abuser may be dead, or he may be living somewhere totally unconcerned about the wounds he inflicted on you. When he greets you he may act as if nothing happened. There are a thousand different situations that can never be unraveled. You have only one recourse if you are to be emotionally whole: You must turn all of these matters over to God—you must completely separate yourself from the burden of seeing these matters resolved on earth. Some people can do this; others cannot.

Your trust in God will grow. Because God did not defend or avenge you when you were abused, you may say, "I can never trust Him." But trust Him you must. Both your past and your future must be left in His hands. No one can ever make peace with their cruel earthly father until they have made peace with their loving heavenly Father.

If you ask why God did not intervene when you were abused, I cannot answer. What if He wanted to show you that He can make someone emotionally whole despite his or her past? What if He wanted to prove that some people will continue to love Him whether He rescues them from their tormentors or not? These matters are hidden in His secret counsels. He is the God who wounds, but He also heals (Deuteronomy 32:39). The fact that He loves you and cares for you is clear in Scriptures. The whys and wherefores are less so. *Confidence in God is absolutely essential to emotional healing.*

Step #3: *Close your past — with Christ*

God is able to take your memories of the past and break their power. As you relive your pain in His presence, you will eventually find it unnecessary to recall the details. The emotional blocks will begin to fall away and there will be healing.

If you broke your arm, God could heal it instantly. It is more likely, however, that it would take several weeks or months. Healing a broken heart is also a process, not an event, but Christ is there to cause your open wound to become merely a scar — healing will have taken place.

God can turn victims into survivors.

He heals the brokenhearted,
And binds up their wounds (Psalm 147:3).

6

THE DARKER SIDE OF EVIL

Satan's doorways, Satan's strategy, and Satan's defeat

WHEN WE CONFRONT our own sins, and the injustices done against us, we soon come into conflict with the spirit world. The deeper the emotional scars, the more power the enemy has over us. All evil is dark, but there is no darkness like that of demonic spirits who want to keep us chained to a painful past. Satan and his legions want to drive the stakes of bitterness, guilt and insecurity in so deeply that we can never pull them out.

Satan himself is not omnipresent; he can be in only one place at one time. He has thousands of demons under his command, though, and they are forced to help him do his dirty work. There is no launching pad used against us in battle more often than the sins and hurts of bygone days.

Robert Louis Stevenson, in his classic *Dr. Jekyll and Mr. Hyde*, concluded that man is not really one but two personalities. He surmised that if these two selves could be housed in separate identities, life would be relieved of all that was unbearable. The unjust side of our nature could go its way delivered from the aspirations of its twin; the just nature could do good without being exposed to shame and the conflict with evil. Stevenson said the curse of mankind was that "these incongruous fagots were bound together."

Our evil side lurks beneath the surface. At the slightest provocation it can erupt unexpectedly into actions that surprise even ourselves. This would be bad enough, but unfortunately, our evil side also is strengthened by those alien satanic forces vying for respect and control.

If you were in a war but didn't know it, it would be unlikely you could conquer your enemy. One of the basic principles of effective warfare is to know your opponent well and to anticipate his strategy.

It is also unfortunate that we have no choice about being in conflict with Satan. To declare neutrality would be equivalent to unconditional surrender. Yet, alas, that is the condition of many Christians today. Some are so ignorant of Satan they think they can be neutral, not realizing that all of us are in a war that must be fought to the finish. Little wonder we are being overrun by the enemy!

Even relatively small decisions which lead us astray may reflect the power of Satan to influence human thoughts. Anger, deceit, immorality, and a host of other sins begin with a series of "innocent" rationalizations. We are at war, not just within ourselves, but also with an antagonist, a cruel and malicious being who seeks our destruction. He hates God and takes out his anger on the whole human race, particularly the people of God. He has tens of thousands of demons under his control who are organized in a hierarchy with accountability structures. These legions have declared war on us.

SATAN'S DOORWAYS

We all know some of the symptoms of demon possession — violent anger, desire to curse God, voices that tell the victim to commit suicide, etc. We sometimes overlook the fact that Satan also works in subtle ways through the human mind to gain control over the human soul.

He seeks a bridge to the mind, a reason *(excuse* is a better word) to gain the measure of control he desires. He can use our past sins and negative emotions to gain a foothold. Obviously, he cannot simply move in on a person without finding at least a crack in the door, or some alibi for covert influence. There are a number of points of entry.

Let's look at some of the doors of the soul that Satan pries open to exert his destructive influence.

The story of Ananias and Sapphira is found in Acts 5. Their friends sold property and gave the entire proceeds to the church. Ananias and Sapphira decided they would do the same, but with one important difference. They chose to give the impression they were donating the entire amount received from their land when, in fact, they were giving only a part of it.

Withholding some of the price was not the issue; they rightly could have kept it all for themselves. The *impression* they wanted to make that they were giving it all was sinful. A rather harmless white lie, we may think.

Yet the apostle Peter, speaking for God, viewed it differently: "Why has Satan filled your heart to lie to the Holy Spirit?" (Acts 5:3). Obviously, Satan was the one who gave them the idea of making themselves appear more spiritual than they really were!

Dishonesty gives Satan an entrance into our lives. *Behind the lie is the liar.*

Fear also can provide an entry for satanic attack. We all have blown wonderful opportunities to witness without ever thinking that our fear may have been inspired by Satan. Yet even before Peter put distance between himself and Christ because of fear, Christ pinpointed the cause:

> Simon, Simon, behold, Satan has demanded permission to sift you like wheat; but I have prayed for you, that your faith may not fail; and you, when once you have turned again, strengthen your brothers (Luke 22:31,32).

Some people live with fear of crowds, fear of sickness and fear of failure. Though some of these can be explained as human weaknesses, Satan strengthens their power to afflict these people. Fear has torment.

The Scriptures link Satan with sexual temptation, doctrinal heresy and spiritual blindness. Whenever we present the Word of God, it always opposes satanic powers.

Of particular interest in this chapter is the fact that Satan can exploit all of our negative feelings, thoughts and behaviors. If you suffered abuse as a child, he may have magnified your fears, pain and anger. Thus many who begin to confront their past find demonic spirits who resist being identified and routed. As the emotional and spiritual healing progresses, Satan finds his cover blown. So of course he contests the steps to freedom.

A story in Mark 9 indicates that demonic spirits may stay in family lines. A distraught father came to Christ with his son who was made mute and frequently thrown to the ground by an evil spirit. Before Christ cast the demon out, He asked the father how long this had been going on. The father answered, "From childhood" (v. 21).

Clearly this little one had not committed any sin to cause a demon to inhabit him. Probably there had been, maybe even still was, occultic activity in his family, and he was a victim of this influence. I believe that spirits desire to perpetuate the sins of the ancestors.

Cultists sometimes sell their children to Satan or put them under a curse, and this often causes their children to be demonized. This satanic affliction must be removed in order for these children to make progress emotionally and spiritually. With today's rise of occult books and paraphernalia, Satan is now being invited into the lives of many unsuspecting teenagers and adults. To watch occult movies, to play games such as Dungeons and Dragons, or to receive information from astrology or Ouija boards—these or any of dozens of other practices can lead to various levels of demonic control.

Deep *feelings of rejection* are also used by Satan to hold people in emotional and spiritual bondage. Recently I spoke with a woman who had been abused as a child. She told me it was difficult to relate with men who were kind to her; abuse she could accept, but not kindness. Like most women who have been victimized, she believed she was so unworthy of true love that she had to reject it when it came her way.

No emotional wounds cut as deeply as rejection or the feelings of *anger* and *worthlessness* that come from various kinds of mistreatment. If you simply harden your heart toward others, you may avoid pain in the future, but you will not find emotional wholeness. If you are *bitter* toward God, these feelings will lead to *despair*. Satan the destroyer will take you to the pit of *depression* and try to get you to commit suicide.

Satan capitalizes on these negative emotions. He lies not just with words but also with feelings. He makes us sense that we are unworthy of love and unworthy of God's mercy or acceptance. Those feelings of rejection and condemnation can drive anyone to despair.

As Christians we have a new identity in Christ— we are accepted in the beloved one—but Satan keeps us blinded from these realities. Through the avenue of our emotions we are tempted to focus on the pain of the past. This causes us to look to ourselves for our sense of wellbeing, and we lose the battle.

SATAN'S STRATEGY

Satan takes several steps in his campaign to possess a human soul. These stages are not necessarily consecutive, nor are they clearly defined, but those who have observed people under the oppression of Satan can discern these levels of satanic involvement.

Stage #1: *Satan begins by injecting into our mind thoughts that we think are our own.*

First, this enables him to *remain hidden while luring us into sin.* This is a brilliant strategy because although sin is attractive to us Satan is not. If he were to appear, telling us what to do, we would be terrified, but because he makes us think these thoughts are ours we have no fear.

Second, this enables him to *work though our existing weaknesses.* He simply takes the sins of the flesh and strengthens their power. There would be alcoholics, adulterers and dishonest people even if Satan did not exist, but he makes these sins more attractive and more powerful. By reinforcing the evil already in the human heart, he can capitalize on our weaknesses without arousing suspicion or fear.

If we welcome these thoughts into our minds, if they find a home in our hearts, he moves in, and on to the second level.

Stage #2: *Now he has a stronghold in which the individual feels compelled to repeat destructive behavior.*

This cycle becomes so strong that no amount of rationalization will change it. Satan has his foot in the door, and the victim feels powerless to close it. No matter how many vows are made to change, when the conditions are right, the behavior is repeated.

Stage #3: *The next level is an obsession which consumes the person.*

It may be the desire for revenge – some people are completely preoccupied with retaliation and anger. They lie awake at night fantasizing about what they would like to do to even the score. Others are preoccupied with covetousness, moral impurity, various addictions or destructive habits. They feel oppressed, unable to find a way out of their sinful thought patterns and behavior.

These thoughts and desires are in the obsessed person's mind almost every waking moment. At this level there may be compulsive behavior, uncontrolled passions for various drugs, lack of sexual restraint, and/or serious eating disorders.

Whenever such a person wishes to make some progress in the Christian life, this obsession is a barrier – a seemingly insurmountable barrier – to progress, always there, beneath the surface, waiting to rear its ugly head.

Bear in mind that many of these thoughts and behaviors would be found on planet earth even if Satan did not exist, but he is the one who exploits these sins and entrenches them so that they become more powerful and compulsive. His goal is stage #4, which is total control.

Stage #4: *At this point demonic spirits actually invade, or take up residence in, the human body.*

There are different levels of demonization; thus the extent of the demonic control varies with each circumstance. Now the person feels *owned* by satanic powers, and in extreme instances may be overcome by supernatural physical strength. The vocal cords may be controlled by these alien powers. There is withdrawal, compulsiveness and self-inflicted torture (see Mark 5:1-9).

Stages 1 and 2 described above usually can be successfully fought by individual Christians. If we repent, memorize God's Word, put on the armor of God and fill our lives with music that praises the Lord, the enemy's power will be severely restricted.

However, either stage 3 or 4 almost always necessitates help from other believers. Jesus taught that some spirits did not go out except by prayer and fasting.

There is a debate among theologians as to whether a demonic spirit can actually inhabit a Christian. Since there are different interpretations of demonization, this question could lead to a lengthy discussion, much beyond the scope of this chapter. So let me simply say here that Christians who have been invaded before their conversion often give evidence that the evil spirits have not left at conversion. Whether or not this should be termed demon possession is disputed. At any rate, we may be certain of this: Christians can experience stages 1 through 3 as outlined above.[1]

Satan's basic method is to increase his control in the lives of his victims. He is willing to do it quickly if he can, but he will do it slowly if he must. He always will go as far as he is able—he will go until he is stopped.

How does Satan hold the ground he has conquered? By using various lies or distortions of truth. He resists any challenge to his authority, but fortunately for us, he must eventually concede to those who understand how to claim the victory of Christ.

SATAN'S MOST CHERISHED LIES

He was a murderer from the beginning, and does not stand in the truth, because there is no truth in him. Whenever he speaks a lie, he speaks from his own nature; for he is a liar, and the father of lies (John 9:44).

The father of lies uses lies to the best advantage.

Handcuffs are made in such a way that if you try to get free, they only become tighter. The struggle tightens the control one more notch. That is also Satan's hope—that when we challenge his authority we will be intimidated and become convinced that we are worse off than ever. Because he fears a challenge, he wants to frighten us. The plan is to make us feel so intimidated we will not even attempt a challenge. If he can make the walls of our own private prison seem formidable, if he can make us believe that the best we can do is adjust to defeat, then he has won the battle before it even begins.

Here are some of the lies he puts in our minds to try to keep us under his control.

Lie #1: *"God cannot give me a new identity."*

We are created in the image of God and as such have a derived value. Christ affirmed the value of a single soul when He asked, "What will a man be profited, if he gains the whole world, and forfeits his soul? Or what will a man give in exchange for his soul?" (Matthew 16:26). Man is the crown of God's creation and has been endowed with glory and honor. If there should be any doubt about the priority God gives to man, we only have to look at the high cost that was paid for our redemption.

Satan hates the attention God gives us and therefore wants to undercut our value. He strikes at the heart of personhood, causing us to doubt whether God could ever love us. He exploits the guilt and the shame, accusing us day and night before the throne.

"Damn you! Nobody could ever love you! You are not worthy to be called a child of God! Can't you see that even God has given up on you?"

These are the words (sometimes even heard audibly) pounding in the minds of those who have a smudged past. The goal is to keep these people looking within themselves, staring at their own private hell and not seeing a way of escape.

Notice: Of course we are sinful and unworthy of God's mercy and grace. We must be convicted of sin to believe the gospel and be saved. Yet, whereas God points out our sin to lead us to His forgiveness and grace, (here is the deception) Satan does so that we might be consigned to a shameful prison of condemnation and worthlessness.

Lie #2: *"God does not love me."*

"Indeed, has God said, 'You shall not eat from any tree of the garden'?" (Genesis 3:1). These are the first words Satan ever spoke to a human being—words that questioned the reputation of God.

Ever since, Satan has been trying to get us to believe God does not have our best interest at heart; God is not trustworthy and does not love us. He points to all the pain in the world, the abuse, the starvation and the suffering, and he asks, "You call this love?"

Every one of us has, at some time, been disappointed with God. Some wonder why He did not intervene when they were abused; others question whether He cares that His people (and for that matter the world) must endure the mental and physical cruelty they experience every moment of the day. Even those of us who were brought up in good homes see the pain in the world and ask: If this is love, who needs it?

The disappointment easily can become resentment, anger and deep-seated hostility. Thus we turn away from God's healing and help. And for that we pay a high price: We are undelivered from our bondage and the scars of the past.

Two consequences follow:

(1) Because we do not believe that God loves us, we cannot trust Him.

This lack of trust then means we cannot take advantage of His promises. Through casting doubt on God's character, Satan keeps people from seeking the Lord who can deliver them. He wants them to picture God as making impossible demands on His creatures—demands that only a few people can meet. God, Satan says, doles out forgiveness only grudgingly; He is unapproachable by those who have committed great sins and whose problems are severe. Many people are driven away from their source of help, the one who can set them free. Or,

(2) *Satan will magnify the sin and shame and make it appear as if God cannot wipe the slate clean.*

If he can make a person's sin problem look bad enough, that person is left with the distinct impression that the problem is so great even God cannot cleanse him.

Recently I counseled a young woman who had been molested by a neighbor at the age of seven. She bore this secret alone for many years. Now in her early twenties, she finally told a friend. When she came to me she wept uncontrollably. "That man stole something from me I can never regain!"

Understandably, she was angry and so was I. Something precious had been taken from her. Yet I had to point out that God could restore her virginity, spiritually speaking. God was able to cleanse her conscience and take away the shame.

This leads us to another lie Satan likes to tell.

Lie #3: *"My problem is too big for God."*

Satan attempts to dethrone God in our thinking by making our problems look bigger than they really are. The intention, of course, is to make it appear that we are beyond hope. Thus, through various fears, people feel spiritually paralyzed, unable to take so much as one step in the direction of freedom.

Notice how deceptive Satan is. Before we commit a sin, he tells us that the matter is small and we will be able to handle any negative fallout. Once the sin has been committed, he makes it look so big that we think not even God has the power to deal with it.

I'm told that out in the wild, two bull moose often will fight for control of a herd. Once a victor has emerged, his authority is never contested by the other again. The loser submits for the rest of his life.

Satan wants to win a few decisive victories so we will serve him without questioning his authority. Just the reminder of losing will be enough to frighten us into submission.

We must contest that authority. Once we see how completely Satan has been defeated, we will take heart. The head of the serpent has been crushed by the One who is seated above all principalities and powers.

How can we overcome these lies? By listening to what God says. Satan and his forces are helpless when faced with truth. "You shall know the truth, and the truth shall make you free" (John 8:32).

SATAN'S DEFEAT

There is a way out. It may not be easy, but it is sure. Thousands who have been bound by Satan can testify that they are free. Here are some principles that must be practiced repeatedly to bring relief from the wiles of the devil.

Complete Submission

All of us can quote the verse: "Resist the devil and he will flee from you," yet we often overlook its context. James writes that God is opposed to the proud but gives grace to the humble. Then he continues, "Submit therefore to God. Resist the devil and he will flee from you. Draw near to God and He will draw near to you" (James 4:6-8).

Before we can resist, we must submit.

This means (a) that we must repent of the sin that gives Satan his foothold. Repentance cuts the ground out from under him. He can no longer hide behind the sin he inspired us to commit.

Then (b) we must submit all of our emotional scars to Christ. That means giving God the hurts that are of our own making as well as those inflicted by others.

In this way we can begin to take back the territory that has been occupied by satanic forces. Often there must be a specific renunciation of sins, memories and strongholds (addictions, compulsions, etc.) that keep us bound.

Because Satan's strategy always involves lies, the only way he can be fought is with transparent honesty. If there is deceit in our lives or an unwillingness to confess the *whole* truth, evil forces will hold their ground. When we repent with the full intention of committing the same sin again, demonic forces have actually been known to use this anticipated sin as grounds for harassment. We slide into the control of Satan through a lie; the only way out is through the truth.

Complete Authority

Is there any doubt in your mind that Christ totally defeated Satan? Is there even a question about who has come out the victor?

Christ's ascension is proof of His infinite superiority over satanic forces: "When He had disarmed the rulers and authorities, He made a public display of them, having triumphed over them through Him" (Colossians 2:15).

Christ's victory is unquestioned, but what about ours? We seem to have mixed results as we confront Satan. Yet we too can look down from heaven, viewing the conflict from Christ's vantage point, because we are "seated . . . with Him in the heavenly places, in Christ Jesus" (Ephesians 2:6).

We can participate in Christ's triumph because we are "in Him." This means we have been granted complete authority — Christ's authority — over evil forces. Little wonder Satan does not want us to see ourselves in heaven; he prefers that we see ourselves as earthbound with no resources for the spiritual battle.

Yes, the roaring lion seeks whom he may devour, but he is *declawed and defanged!* To us he appears powerful, but to God he is insignificant.

Complete Armor

This is not the place to explain all the pieces of armor listed in Ephesians 6. We just need to realize they are necessary for both our protection and our spiritual advancement.

For example, the shield of faith extinguishes "all the flaming missiles of the evil one," and the sword of the Spirit that enables us to move forward is "the word of God." When Christ confronted Satan, He quoted the Word: "It is written . . . " (see Matthew 4:1-11). That is the pattern we must follow in resisting temptation and expelling Satan's thoughts and influence.

Complete Accountability

No one can live the Christian life alone, simply because a war is never won by one person. There has to be unity, mutual dependence and interrelated strategy. To stand against Satan, we need to understand warfare praying (to be discussed in the next chapter), and we need others who can counsel those bound by the chains of Satan.

We need other believers to help us in the fight.

Complete Preparation

How do we prepare for temptation? A young man who had the pornography habit told me how often he would vow to give up this practice only to succumb again and again. I knew there was no use asking him to promise he would not repeat this behavior, but I did ask him to make a promise of a different kind: to memorize five verses of Scripture, and when he was tempted, to quote each of these verses five times, preferably out loud. He made the promise, and he went to work.

It was not long before he faced a powerful temptation. By mistake a pornographic magazine was delivered to his mailbox. He contemplated opening it but remembered his promise. So, out loud, he began to quote the verses, five times each. By the time he was finished, he was able to destroy the magazine without opening it.

Of course, there are battles; some behavioral trenches are deep and the wounds of the past are still painful. But there is a path to victory and freedom if we are willing to wage the war.

A boy was jumping up and down with excitement on a baseball diamond. A man walking by asked, "What is the score?"

"We are losing 23-0!" came the surprising reply.

"If you are losing, why are you so excited?"

"Well, we haven't been to bat yet!"

You may have just come through a string of losses—but Christ is able to put you back into the ball game. With His strength you can hit some balls over the fence for home runs!

Only ignorance would make us surrender to an enemy who has already been defeated. The darkness of the past dissipates in the presence of the One who is light and truth.

But there is still more to learn.

7

CHANNELING GOD'S POWER

Four characteristics of effective prayer

BACK IN 1968, several other young men and I climbed to the top of Masada, the massive fortification in Israel near the southern end of the Dead Sea. It took us several hours in 100 + degree temperature to make it to the top (most tourists now go up in a cable car). By climbing it ourselves, we better understood why the Roman armies were unable to capture the Jews who occupied the top of this fortification. Whenever the Romans tried to scale the mountain, they were beaten back by the Jews who often would simply let rocks roll down on them.

Though greatly outnumbered and with few resources, the Jews lived on the top of the mountain for more than three years before they were starved out by the Romans.

Masada is a stronghold, most likely the fortification referred to as the "strongholds of Engedi" (1 Samuel 23:29). Whoever occupied it had a tremendous advantage over the enemy. All the odds were against the attackers who found it nigh impossible to scale the mountain with its walls and defenses. Little wonder the Romans simply chose to wait until the Jews were out of food.

The conflict of Masada teaches us **two important principles of warfare.**

First, *it is much easier to defend territory in our possession than to recapture it after it has gone into the hands of the enemy.*

The Jews kept the Romans at bay for several years, but once Rome captured the fortress, there was not the slightest chance the Jews could have regained possession of it.

The analogy is clear: It is much easier to defend our lives from Satan than it is to take territory back that we have lost to him. To say no to alcohol is easy when you have never tasted it, but it is much more difficult once it has become a part of your lifestyle. Those who struggle with overeating know how difficult it is to take some pounds off—how much better never to have put them on!

However powerful sexual temptation may be, its attraction will become still stronger after we give in to it. Every time we say yes to our lusts we develop a natural momentum to say yes later on.

This principle is a powerful reminder that the best (and easiest) time to say no to a sinful lifestyle is when it is first presented to us. No matter how fierce the struggle, every loss means the struggle ahead will be even greater. For every inch we give to Satan, he wants a yard. And every inch we wish to recapture involves serious confrontation with the enemy.

Many of you reading these pages have long since left the days when your life was free from enemy control. Satan (in league with the flesh) has occupied a considerable part of your body and mind for some time. You must recapture the territory that is behind enemy lines.

The same applies to those of you who were abused in your past; the part of you that is ruining your future needs to be reclaimed for the glory of God. The fortresses that hold past memories and feelings must be vacated to make room for the new ownership.

Second, Masada teaches us that
to capture enemy fortifications *we must have
weapons and personnel equal to the task.*

Even if the enemy is relatively weak, when he is in a good position he can do a lot of damage. If he has entrenched himself, built buttresses and dug deep foundations, you are set for a long battle. He insists he will not budge, no matter what.

How do we recapture territory that is in enemy hands? How is it possible to go behind enemy lines, dislodge the bulwarks and route the adversary? How can we plant Christ's flag of victory on territory presently in the midst of enemy occupation?

The answer: through strong, aggressive prayer. We must be able to access the power of God and focus the victory of Christ directly on the strongholds of the mind and the emotions. This is not the time for general petitions ("please bless John"); it is the time for strategic warfare with artillery directed toward key targets. We're talking about bombing the ramparts; we are speaking of assaulting the foe and engaging him in direct combat. We are crossing enemy lines, naming the opposing warriors and taking authority over the intruders. We are in it to win.

This kind of prayer enables us to channel the power of God. We take the victory of the cross, resurrection and ascension and apply it to specific areas of our lives. Through prayer, God's power can halt the setbacks of the past and give hope for the future.

Some New Agers tell us that certain gifted individuals called channelers can tap into spiritual power and communicate with "masters of wisdom" who lived on the earth many years ago. They are quite right in insisting there is a spiritual dimension to the universe, but unfortunately they are plugged in to the wrong spirit world.

However, I am not prepared to surrender the word *channeling* to the New Agers. Christians are channelers too—channelers for the power of God. Remember the song, "Channels Only"? Just as a television set can be tuned to different channels, so we can be tuned to God's frequency, and when that happens lives are permanently changed.

How can we pray in such a way that we will see the unmistakable evidence of changed lives? How can the wounds of the past be healed and the future be made productive?

OBSTACLES TO EFFECTIVE PRAYER

After Paul listed the armor of God that all of us must wear if we are to be successful against the enemy, he added:

> With all prayer and petition pray at all times in the Spirit, and with this in view, be on the alert with all perseverance and petition for all the saints (Ephesians 6:18).

This kind of praying has several characteristics which we will examine, but first we must deal with two obstacles, two mental barriers, that keep us from meaningful prayer.

The **first** mental barrier is that *we honestly doubt whether God cares.*

After all, if He really were as concerned as the Bible seems to teach, where is He when we are sick, when we lose our jobs, or when our family falls apart? As we have already learned, children who have been abused have a difficult time trusting in the care of God.

This is not an easy barrier to overcome, but many people who have been abused or who have suffered injustices have come to grips with their distrust of God and found Him to be a reliable friend. David wrote, "He does not forget the cry of the afflicted" (Psalm 9:12).

I urge you to come to God with your spiritual and emotional bruises and with your misgivings, and you will find that He does heal the brokenhearted and give comfort to those who mourn. Don't think you have to resolve all your doubts and misgivings before you come.

When we get past the first mental barrier, we often discover a **second** one, the one that keeps us off our knees: the thorny problem of *the will of God.*

The Bible says if we ask according to His will, He hears us, but the sixty-four-dollar question is, How do I know what His will is? We've all thought we knew God's will and prayed accordingly — only to be disappointed. So we gave up, reasoning, "If it is God's will, He will do it whether or not I pray; if it is not God's will, He is not going to do it no matter how hard I pray — so what's the use?"

The net result is that we often pray in unbelief. We mention various matters to God but would be shocked if we saw an answer. We are not convinced He cares, and we don't want to waste energy that will not get results.

In John Bunyan's *Pilgrim's Progress* a young woman and her children are seen knocking on the Wicket Gate. In a moment a ferocious dog begins to bark, making the woman and children afraid. They face a dilemma: If they continue to knock, they must fear the dog; if they turn away, the gatekeeper will be offended and they will not be admitted. They continue to knock, ever so fervently. Finally, they hear the voice of the gatekeeper asking, "Who is there?" and instantly the dog ceases barking.

The moment we are serious about prayer a thousand dogs begin to bark. If we listen to them, we will turn away. If we continue to knock, we will hear the voice of our Master and we will be encouraged to press on.

FOUR CHARACTERISTICS
OF EFFECTIVE PRAYER

In the next few pages we will discuss some of the characteristics of effective prayer—but it is up to each individual to put the principles into practice.

1. We Must Pray in God's Will

When we pray for a promotion, or that a child will be healed, or that God would give us a marriage partner, the question of the will of God always emerges as a part of the picture. In instances like these we must end our prayer with, "If it be Thy will."

On the other hand, there are some requests we can make with absolute certainty that we are praying in His will. We can pray powerfully, without a hint of unbelief. We can pray with boldness and confidence—no need to waffle about the will of God. For example, Paul prayed for the believers in Ephesus:

> I pray that the eyes of your heart may be enlightened, so that you may know what is the hope of His calling, what are the riches of the glory of His inheritance in the saints, and what is the surpassing greatness of His power toward us who believe (Ephesians 1:18,19).

That is the will of God for every believer. No wonder Paul could pray with such confidence!

A second example is Colossians 1:9-12 where he prays that the believers will have *seven special qualities:*

(1) Knowing the will of God.

This has to do with the wisdom that we need to make decisions, the ability to distinguish the good from the best and the false from the true.

(2) Walking worthy of the Lord.

This means that we live lives that are a credit to Christ. The word *worthy* means "weighty"; that is, our lives should make a lasting, indelible impression. Some people's lives are like the sand that is soon washed away. In the end there is nothing left. Paul prayed that the Colossian Christians would live in such a way as to make a permanent impact on others.

(3) Bearing fruit in every good work.

This quality involves spiritual productivity. We will bear either good fruit or evil fruit. The fruit that we allow God to develop in our lives will remain. It will not rot when the sun beats on it.

(4) Increasing in the knowledge of God.

The pinnacle of all intellectual and spiritual experience is knowing God. We should pray that people would have an increasing understanding of His attributes and of their relationship with Him.

(5) Being strengthened spiritually.

The source for this is nothing less than "His glorious might."

(6) Attaining spiritual stability.

We need steadfastness and patience when we encounter the various trials of life.

(7) Giving thanks.

Paul viewed this characteristic as particularly important because it honors the Father who has qualified us to share in the inheritance of the saints in light.

If you are a woman, think of what it would be like to be married to a man who has all of these qualities! If you are a man, think of having a wife like this!

This is a picture of a person who is emotionally and spiritually whole. Here is one who is no longer a slave to the past, nor held hostage to any damaging effects of a dysfunctional family. Is there any doubt in your mind that this is God's will for every Christian? Warfare praying (to be explained more fully later), like these prayers of Paul, can be prayed with *unswerving confidence*. It is praying in line with God's revealed desires. No need to be timid because of uncertainty about God's will.

2. We Must Pray in the Power of the Spirit

The Holy Spirit is deeply involved in all of our active prayer life.

At times each of us wonders why we have to bother to pray. God could take care of our petitions whether we prayed them or not. We pray that God will heal a sick friend or help a friend overcome an addiction. Why does God wait for us to pray before He acts?

Suppose you have a rebellious, strong-willed six-year-old son and you tell him, "Please do not watch TV this afternoon." He disobeys you.

You decide you are going to wait for him to initiate a discussion about his disobedience. To get his attention, you choose not to prepare dinner for him. Six o'clock comes and nothing is on the table. He is too rebellious to ask for something to eat because such a request is a form of submission and he is too independent just yet.

Of course you could go ahead and make supper anyway—you have the power to do so—but you have a different agenda. *The boy's attitude toward his disobedience is of more immediate concern than his hunger.*

Around nine o'clock he grudgingly asks if you could fix him something to eat. You are glad he has made this initial step toward you, but you are still not satisfied. His defiance is at the top of your agenda. He isn't ready for his dinner yet.

Of course God could grant us our requests whether we asked or not, or whether we were in fellowship with Him or not—but He has other priorities. **First**, He wants us to *face all areas of disobedience* when we make a request before Him: "If I regard wickedness in my heart, the Lord will not hear" (Psalm 66:18).

I do not wish to imply that all of our prayers would be answered if we just surrendered our self-will. My point is that God wants us to pray before He acts, simply because our personal relationship with Him is so high on His list of priorities.

His **second** priority is *fellowship with us* — His love for us and our love for Him. To pray in the Spirit means we pray in *submission* and *faith,* with no unconfessed sin, and believing that God will respond to us. "Without faith it is impossible to please Him, for he who comes to God must believe that He is, and that He is a rewarder of those who seek Him" (Hebrews 11:6). Thus, in faith, we receive the Spirit's power for effective prayer.

There are some things God will not do until His people pray. As already mentioned, He could act whether we pray or not, and sometimes He does. Yet most important is our attitude toward Him; He wants us to have fellowship with Him. This is number one on His list of objectives. Archbishop Trench said, "Prayer is not overcoming God's reluctance; it is laying hold of His highest willingness."

We come with our need for health, money and other blessings, and we discover that we have a much greater need: the need for God Himself. The other problems God has allowed in our lives are just vehicles to get us into His presence.

In fact, the Holy Spirit is so vitally concerned about our prayers that in those times when we don't know how to pray — when the hurts are too deep or the matters are too confused — He prays along with us and He intercedes for us:

> And in the same way the Spirit also helps our weakness;
> for we do not know how to pray as we should, but the
> Spirit Himself intercedes for us with groanings too deep for
> words; and He who searches the hearts knows what the

mind of the Spirit is, because He intercedes for the saints according to the will of God (Romans 8:26,27).

Bunyan wrote: "In prayer it is better to have heart without words than words without heart."

What does "praying in the Spirit" mean? It means that we pray in harmony with God. We are not coming with a request simply because we have been pushed into a corner. We are coming to ask, but also to love, to fellowship, and to enjoy God. Then the Holy Spirit guides us in our prayer life.

Why not pray right now and ask the Holy Spirit to give you wisdom and guidance in your prayer life? Sometimes we have not because we ask not.

3. We Must Pray in the Name of Christ

Truly, truly, I say to you, if you shall ask the Father for anything, He will give it to you in My name. Until now you have asked for nothing in My name; ask, and you will receive, that your joy may be made full (John 16:23,24).

Why did Christ insist that all prayer had to be in His name? Simply put, we do not have the qualifications we need to approach God, much less receive answers from Him. Here we are totally dependent on Christ's credentials. Through His name we receive:

(1) The access of Christ.

Obviously Christ is in God's presence, and when we pray in His name we are in God's presence too. It's not just that God hears us, but He also welcomes us—Christ has ushered us into the presence of the King.

(2) The authority of Christ.

The subject of this chapter is how to destroy strongholds—to demolish the power of the enemy. We've learned that effective warfare means we have the resources not just to resist the enemy, but also to rout him from his entrenched positions. This can be done only in the name of someone stronger than Satan, stronger than our past, our sins and our memories.

In chapter 6, I emphasized the victory of Christ over the world of evil spirits. There can be no doubt in our minds about the fact that Satan has been crushed. To pray in Christ's name is to apply His victory boldly in a specific situation.

When Edmund Gravely died at the controls of his small plane, his wife kept the plane aloft for two hours. She radioed for help and her distress signal was picked up, but communication was impossible because she kept changing channels. Eventually she made a rough landing, but it would have been so much easier if she had stayed tuned to the right frequency.

There is only one way to see answers to prayer and that is to stay tuned to the right channel all day. Every single situation must be brought before our heavenly Father with confidence in the name of the Lord Jesus Christ.

4. We Must Confront the Enemy

Standing against Satan to undo the damage he has caused is not easy, but it is both necessary and rewarding. The strategy, remember, is to go behind enemy lines to subdue and dislodge him and to send him fleeing.

Remember these simple rules:

(1) Get suited up for the battle.

We must make sure we are ready for the battles that will face us the minute we are serious about taking authority over the enemy. We must be dressed for the occasion. Through prayer we must put on the "whole armor of God." Mark Bubeck in his helpful book, *The Adversary,* gives an example of the kind of prayer that suits us for battle:

> Heavenly Father, I desire to be obedient by being strong in the Lord and the power of Your might. I see

this is Your will and purpose for me. I recognize it is essential to put on the armor You have provided, and I do so now with gratitude and praise because You have provided all I need to stand in victory against Satan and his kingdom. Grant me wisdom to discern the tactics and sneakiness of Satan's strategy against me. Enable me to gain victory as I wrestle the princes, powers, rulers, and wicked spirits who carry the battle against me.

I delight to take the armor You have provided and by faith to put it on as effective protection against the spiritual forces of darkness.

I confidently take the loin-girdle of truth that You offer me. I take Him who is the truth as my strength and protection. I reject Satan's lies and deceiving ways to gain advantage against me. Grant me wisdom to recognize the subtle ways in which Satan seeks to cause me to accept His lies as truth . . .[1]

The prayer continues, listing all the pieces of armor, affirming each in faith and accepting each as protection against Satan's strategy. In this way we can arm ourselves for the conflict.

Where territory has been given over to Satan, specific sins must be renounced. Often believers fail to realize it is possible for a sin that has been forgiven to still have control over an individual. Breaking the power of cancelled sin, as Charles Wesley put it, is essential.

Enlisting the prayer support of other believers is also necessary if spiritual hindrances (strongholds) are to be overcome and torn down.

(2) Begin to pray for others.

We can now start taking back the ground that another individual has given to the enemy. Again, Bubeck gives an example of that kind of prayer. The following is a helpful summary.

Loving heavenly Father, in the name of our Lord Jesus Christ, I bring before You (name of other person) in prayer. I ask for guidance that I might pray in the Spirit as You have told me. In the name of the Lord Jesus

Christ and as a priest of God, I ask for mercy and forgiveness for the sins by which (name) has grieved You. I claim back the ground of his life which he has given to Satan by believing the enemy's deception. In the name of Christ I resist all of Satan's activity to hold (name) in blindness and darkness. I pull down the strongholds formed against (name). I destroy all the plans formed against his mind, his will, his emotions, and his body.

I claim (name) for You in the name of the Lord Jesus Christ and I thank You for the answer to my prayer. In the name of the Lord Jesus Christ. Amen.[2]

In those cases where the person is cooperating with you in prayer, you might want to give specific instructions as to how to pray — developing the concepts of confession, the power we have through our union with Christ, and praise for spiritual victory.

This kind of praying eventually will overcome the resistance of the enemy. Warfare praying is like pounding the walls of a stronghold with artillery designed to smash those walls. Through this kind of believing prayer we can indeed go behind enemy lines and take back ownership that has either willingly or unwillingly been given to the enemy.

How long do we need to pray before we see results? Sometimes there are immediate changes; sometimes it takes longer.

Fasting should also become a part of this kind of intercession. Today when we call a feast, everyone comes, even those whom we have not seen in years. But when we call a fast, the attendance is meager, if anyone shows up at all. Yet Christ assumed we would exercise this discipline:

And when you fast, do not put on a gloomy face as the hypocrites do, for they neglect their appearance in order to be seen fasting by men. Truly I say to you, they have their reward in full (Matthew 6:16).

Although the disciples had great success casting out demons, there was one particularly stubborn one. The victim was a young boy, and an evil spirit kept throwing him into the fire or into the water. The disciples could not cast the demon out. Christ rebuked them for their unbelief, and later, when the disciples asked why they couldn't cast it out, Christ answered, "This kind does not go out except by prayer and fasting" (Matthew 17:21).

Perseverance is a word we need to hear often in these days of pop religion and instant solutions. Nothing will accomplish permanent results like persistent, bold, authoritative prayer. Prevailing prayer wins great victories, but the outcome should never be taken for granted. Only when we are under Christ's authority can we exercise that authority as His representatives.

We know that we have destroyed a fortress when there is *nothing in ourselves (or others for whom we pray) that belongs to the enemy.*

Keeping our eyes on God and our artillery on the enemy is the sure path to victory.

> The effective prayer of a righteous man
> can accomplish much (James 5:16).

8

FINDING YOUR WAY BACK

*It's never too late to
turn around*

TAKING A WRONG ROAD sometimes has dire consequences.

Four of us learned that the hard way back in 1974. Our friends had invited us to spend a few days with them in their new home in Northern Wisconsin. One evening, in the dead of winter, they decided to take us out for dinner to a restaurant in a small secluded town about ten miles away. Though new in the area, they had confidence they could find it without any trouble.

About five miles down the road they became increasingly convinced that we were on the wrong country road. The car made fresh, deep ruts in the snow; the farther we went, the deeper the snow, and the more bleak the surroundings. Clearly we were headed for no-man's land.

On and on we drove until we came to a crossroad where we attempted a turn-around. We were stuck in the snow for about an hour and a half in zero degree temperature, but eventually we managed to get the vehicle back on the road and headed for home.

A wrong turn on the road of life is also hazardous, fraught with numerous unhappy consequences.

King David illustrates what can happen when we turn at a wrong corner. You recall that he committed adultery with Bathsheba and then murdered her husband as part of a cover-up. From there his life went from bad to worse.

LESSONS ALONG THE ROAD OF LIFE

There are several parallels between our experience in Northern Wisconsin and those costly detours along the road of life. Here are some lessons that all of us must learn about heading in the wrong direction.

1. We lose time that can never be regained.

We never did get to that restaurant — in fact, my wife and I have not been there to this day. We had wasted so much time on the wrong road that it was too late to go out to eat; we were just glad we made it home where we could enjoy a bowl of hot soup.

The lesson of wrong roads was a costly one for David — he lost several years of service for his Lord thanks to the wrong turns he made on his earthly journey. He never could make up for the lost time.

Live for yourself, and you can never go back to that day when you got off course. A ticking clock can be thrown into a trash can, and a current calendar can be burned, but time moves relentlessly forward.

2. The ruts we leave can mislead others.

We do not know that the trail we left in the snow sent a misleading signal to other drivers, but it might have.

I can easily imagine someone choosing to follow this road because it looked traveled. Not unreasonably, he could have thought it would lead to the nearby town.

We had the good fortune of turning around and making it back home, but a driver who followed us might not have been that lucky. He could have decided to go several miles farther only to get stuck and be unable to return at all. He could have been stranded in sub-zero temperature for quite a long time.

David repented of the path he had chosen, but his children, who followed him, did not repent of theirs. The two sins of immorality and murder overshadowed his family when he was still alive and continued to do so long after his death. Amnon, David's son, raped his own half-sister Tamar. Absalom committed immorality with his father's mistresses on a rooftop for all to see. Immorality was rampant among his children.

God had said the sword would not depart from David's household, and it didn't. Absalom was slain by David's military leader, and another son, Adonijah, had to be killed because he aspired to take his father's throne.

The story is familiar — a man leaves his wife and children to marry a spurious lover, and years later he comes to repent of his sin. His life is turned around and again headed in God's direction, but the children follow the father's path to its destructive end. He changes his direction, but they do not.

3. The mistake cannot be corrected by taking adjacent roads.

We made a few turns enroute to that little town, but because we were on the wrong road to begin with, making a series of different turns only meant we were getting farther from where we wanted to go.

One fork in the road usually leads to another — and when we first choose a wrong path the next choice also will lead us astray. All roads going in the wrong direction are equally misleading; going from one to another does not get us back on the right path.

To return to King David: After he discovered Bathsheba was pregnant with his child he should have brought Uriah home from battle and admitted candidly what had happened. Then he could have humbly sought Uriah's forgiveness and discussed what his responsibility should be in light of the impending birth of the baby. In this way, David would have repented soon after he took the wrong turn on the highway of life.

But he did what we so often do — he chose to take other paths in a vain attempt to correct his mistake. Unfortunately, those choices only got him further away from where he got off course.

First, he tried plan A. He brought Uriah home from battle and tried to persuade him to go home hoping he would make love with his wife, and thus the identity of the child would be hidden. But Uriah wouldn't go home. He said it was unfair for him to have such a vacation while his comrades were engaged in war.

Plan B. *I'll get Uriah drunk. Maybe he'll go home then. What he won't do sober, he might do drunk.* That scheme didn't work either.

Parenthetically we might ask: Suppose the cover-up had worked — would David have been off the hook? Hardly. Bathsheba knew the truth, David knew the truth, and most important, God knew.

Plan C. David's trump card. *I will have to have Uriah killed.* Then he could take Bathsheba as his wife and everyone (if they could be trusted not to count the months between the wedding and the birth of the baby) would think the child was conceived in wedlock.

So he gave Uriah a sealed note to give to Joab his military commander. It stated that Uriah should be put into the hottest battle, and the other men were to retreat, leaving Uriah to certain death. Joab did as he was asked. Uriah died in battle, and David married Bathsheba.

These decisions actually compounded the original problem. Rather than returning to where he got off course, David's taking these adjacent roads only made it more difficult for him to return. Every mile in the wrong direction meant another mile to cover on the way back.

Of course he could never go back in time, but he could have returned in spirit to where he was before the adultery took place. Eventually he did, but how much better if he had done it sooner rather than later!

Every day we postpone repentance we find ourselves entangled with more sin. Many a knotted mess could be avoided if the participants would only turn around immediately, just as soon as they become conscious of getting off course.

If you need to return to God, *today will be as easy as it will ever get*. Every day you live, turning around becomes more difficult. The more painful your past, the harder it is to contemplate turning to God. Yet the more necessary it is to do just that.

4. Often there seems no place to turn around.

After we had driven 5 or 6 miles in the deep snow, we debated whether we should turn around—we thought surely the road must lead to some village or town, or perhaps there would be a farmhouse just around the corner. We had gone so far that we felt the urge to continue, no matter what. The road became narrower, though, and the snow became deeper. Still there was no sign of civilization. Eventually, it appeared we couldn't turn around if we wanted to.

I've known people who pursue destructive paths with abandon. Some are non-Christians who have shut God out of their lives for many years. Even when they come to die they reject Him. They say, "I have lived without Him; I shall die without Him."

Christians who have been pursuing their own selfish agenda also find it hard to turn around. They have made too many investments along the path of life—they have nursed too many hurts, have sinned too many times, or have felt too much pain. They turn their back toward God and keep going, thinking, *Someday I'll turn around.* Yet no time ever seems convenient, no place ever seems appropriate, and in the end, it is nearly always too late.

David was out of fellowship with God for several months before he was willing to come clean and honestly face his sin and its consequences. In Psalm 32 he describes the agony of those deceptive months:

> When I kept silent about my sin, my body wasted away
> through my groaning all day long.
> For day and night Thy hand was heavy upon me;
> My vitality was drained away as with the fever heat
> of summer (Psalm 32:3,4).

There were two reasons David found it so hard to turn around: (1) His guilt and shame made honest disclosure difficult; and (2) he knew that, even though he would be forgiven, the damage of the past could never be made right.

David knew it did not matter how many tears he shed, Bathsheba's purity could never be restored. No matter how many years he lived with regret, Uriah would never be brought back to life. Forgiveness would not change these consequences. David finally had to realize that only God can put our past behind us. We can only make the mess; we cannot cover it. For that we must turn to the Lord our God.

A woman who had an abortion said she could not receive God's forgiveness because "nothing will ever bring my baby back to me." She had to learn, as David did, that *we must turn around and receive pardon from God, even though the effects of our sin will continue.*

What does it take to turn around? What does it take to change direction, to get back into fellowship with God where you belong?

TAKING THE ROAD BACK TO GOD

Psalm 51 is the cry of a man who finally has chosen to "come clean." David would never have turned to the Almighty unless he knew he would be received and welcomed back into fellowship. In his grief he rediscovered some of the attributes of God that gave him the assurance that the mess he created could be covered. He could take the road back. Those attributes include:

The Mercy of God

In the first verse he uses three different words to describe the mercy of God:

> Be gracious to me, O God, according to Thy lovingkindness; According to the greatness of Thy compassion, blot out my transgressions (Psalm 51:1).

The word *gracious* means "to bestow a favor." David is asking God to give him something he does not deserve, something he has not earned.

Lovingkindness refers to "God's unfailing love." The Hebrew word has the same root as the word *stork*, a bird known for its tender care of its young. David pleads that God will not abandon him, but that He will carefully meet his deepest needs.

The third word, *compassion,* is related to the Hebrew word *womb*. The imagery is of a mother tenderly nursing her newborn. David is saying, "God, please treat me tenderly because I am hurting . . . hold me gently in Your arms and take care of me."

Obviously God now has David's complete attention, and David has God's attention, too. David is tired of traveling in the wrong direction and wants to come back to the warmth of the Father's house where he belongs.

How would David handle the fact that he destroyed so many lives? He made a statement in this prayer that we might be tempted to challenge. He says:

> Against Thee, Thee only, I have sinned.
> And done what is evil in Thy sight,
> So that Thou art justified when Thou dost speak,
> And blameless when Thou dost judge (v. 4, KJV).

We might want to correct David here. He had sinned against Bathsheba and Uriah, not to mention all his other wives to whom he had pledged his allegiance. Why does he say his sin was against God alone?

David understood full well that all sin is first and foremost a violation of the character of God. In the process of sinning against God we happen to hurt other people; but it is with God we have to deal since it is His laws we have broken.

This is important to David for this reason: *He knew he could never be reconciled to those whom he had hurt on earth.* He had betrayed Bathsheba and she might forgive him, but he could never be restored to Uriah.

Sometimes sin causes human relationships to be so completely severed that they can never be rectified on earth. Perhaps your father died when you were a rebellious teenager. How you wish you could have asked his forgiveness for the way you treated him! Or you may have ruined a child's life through abuse, a lack of love, or a bad example. You might wish these things could be made right, but they cannot be. What do you do?

David knew our first obligation is to be reconciled to the supreme lawgiver of the universe and then to commit all of our unfinished business to Him. We recognize that He is completely just in His dealings with us and in the lives of others we have wronged.

The Forgiveness of God

With a pencil, underline all the different terms David uses to refer to God's forgiveness. "Blot out my transgressions." "Wash me thoroughly from mine iniquity." "Cleanse me from my sin." "Purify me." "Hide Thy face from my sins." These are some of the expressions he uses to speak of what he wanted God to do in his heart.

Here was a man who knew both the power of sin and the praises of forgiveness. He believed his sordid past was not too much for God. He could be clean within his heart, where it really mattered.

When he prays, "Create in me a clean heart, O God, and renew a steadfast spirit within me" (v. 10), he is counting on the ability of God to transform him within despite the dreadful circumstances without. Once this miracle was done within, God would open David's lips so his mouth would declare God's praises.

Imagine! David could sing again! No doubt his wives were whispering in anger behind his back when he brought the new first lady Bathsheba into the king's palace. Think of the bitter gossip in David's army when word got out that he had one of his fifty mighty men deliberately killed to cover his adultery! News of the scandal flooded Jerusalem, with the story exaggerated each time it was told. David was the laugh of the town.

Yet, for all that, he would have his joy restored (v. 12), and he would teach other transgressors the ways of God and they would believe (v. 13). Yes, there was hope in the midst of the darkness.

The Providence of God

The mess David had made would not evaporate even though David had now received God's forgiveness. The bitter consequences would always be there—but God delights in bringing good out of evil. A rose would grow up with the thorns.

The levitical law did not prescribe any sacrifice for the sins of murder and adultery. The law specified that the offender was to die. This is why David prayed:

> For Thou dost not delight in sacrifice,
>   otherwise I would give it;
> Thou art not pleased with burnt offering.
>   The sacrifices of God are a broken spirit;
> A broken and a contrite heart, O God,
>   Thou wilt not despise (v. 16,17).

God would not despise that broken and contrite heart. Out of the ashes, some blessing would come.

After Bathsheba became David's wife the child that was conceived in adultery died. David had other children with her, though, and the best known was Solomon.

Strictly speaking, Solomon should never have been born, for Bathsheba should never have become one of David's wives. Yet God is never at a loss in the midst of the wreckage of human failure and sin. God told David that Solomon would be great and would be a special blessing to the people (2 Samuel 12:24,25; 1 Kings 1:37).

Unfortunately, Solomon had two hearts — one to love God and another to love women and wealth. Through it all, (1) he built the Temple that David had wanted to build for God, (2) he wrote thousands of proverbs that became a part of the Word of God, and (3) both he and his mother Bathsheba are listed in the genealogy of Christ found in Matthew 1:6.

Do you recall the story of the beautiful piece of cloth that had some ink accidentally spilled on it? Though the ink could not be removed, an artist painted a picture on it and used the blotch as part of the scenery.

God has had much experience in using our sins to create beauty and value. Indeed, out of the greatest failure of mankind (the sin of Adam and Eve), God brought the greatest display of His mercy and grace in redemption.

REASONS TO TURN AROUND

Let's summarize some lessons David learned. If we have wandered from the path of fellowship, we shall be encouraged to turn around and become fruitful for God once more.

1. It is never too late to turn to God.

It may be harder now than it was in the past, but it is never too late. The time is always appropriate to do what is right. As long as you are alive you still have the capacity to turn around and head in a different direction.

Though our sin may have caused irreparable damage, we should turn to God in repentance and faith. Only He can make the best of the mess.

When we were lost in the winter storm in Northern Wisconsin we looked for a crossroad where we could turn around. God has provided such a place on the road of life. The cross of Christ is the point at which we can reverse our direction and walk in the direction of God. That cross is a reminder that we *can* turn around.

David lived before the cross so did not see God's forgiveness with the clarity we do—but even his sin was eventually laid on Christ. Yes, God says, "Turn around."

2. God can put your past behind you.

What about the memories of our sin? What about the ruts left in the snow? How can we ever be free from the reminders of our failure?

A businessman was notorious for saving everything. His office files were bulging with useless papers he would never look at. His exasperated secretary kept asking him if she could dispose of all the old, useless material. The man was reluctant, but she insisted. "All right," he finally said, "but be sure you photocopy everything before you throw it away!"

When God cleans out your life He doesn't make photocopies; we do. He just throws the files away. Once our sins are blotted out and cast into the depths of the sea we can move forward — in the direction of God. Why should we remember what God has promised to forget? As already emphasized, we must leave the consequences to God. When we have done all we can to repair the damage, God must do the rest. *We do the possible; God does the impossible.*

3. God wants you to look ahead.

He wants you to look through the windshield rather than into the rear-view mirror. Once the direction of your life has changed, there is no use in looking back to a past you have left behind.

It is more important to see where you are going than to be preoccupied with where you have been.

David knew what it was like to slide into the ditch along the path of life, but God lifted him to his feet and set him on the right course:

> He brought me up out of the pit of destruction,
>   out of the miry clay;
> And He set my feet upon a rock
>   making my footsteps firm
> And He put a new song in my mouth,
>   a song of praise to our God;
> Many will see and fear,
>   And will trust in the LORD (Psalm 40:2,3).

Once you have been lifted out of the ditch and set back onto the right road, there is little value in living in the past. God wants to put your past behind you so you can get on with living the rest of your days for His glory.

In the following chapters you will read the stories of some who have allowed God to put their past behind them. Amid their heartaches and grief, these people have found their way home.

You too will be encouraged to change course.

9

ABUSE :
A Personal Testimony

Proof of hope for the sexual abuse victim

SUSAN CALLS HERSELF a survivor, a woman who has been healed of the emotional trauma that comes with sexual abuse.

She was reared in a Christian home by parents who were thought to be models of Christian faithfulness and devotion. Her father was active in Sunday school and displayed qualities of Christian leadership.

When Susan was about six, her father began taking indecent liberties with her. He told her this was merely his way of showing his love for his beautiful daughter. There was nothing to fear; this was just the way people showed they cared for each other.

But Susan knew something was wrong. *Very wrong.* To escape the pain of reality, the little girl drifted into an imaginary world where everything was just right. She had imaginary friends and animals that became real to her and they assured her that everything was really quite fine. The reality of what was happening became fantasy, and the fantasy became her reality.

As an adult, Susan had no idea how deeply her past, buried within the depths of her soul, was affecting her life. All she knew was that it was hard for her to relate to men — just a simple touch caused her to cringe. She also found it difficult to form deep friendships with men or women. She could not let anyone know who she really was. If they knew her past, she thought they would reject her.

For many years Susan felt guilty about what had happened to her. Shame came with the violation of her sexuality. Though she was an unwilling participant, she nevertheless felt it was all her fault.

Only in retrospect did she realize this was false guilt; in reality, she was the victim of a crime. Though she gave in to her father's overtures without a fight, the fact is he had misused his authority. What six-year-old is prepared to reprimand her father whom she loves and respects? This traumatic experience did not diminish her value as a person, nor did it imply a fault in her character. What happened was not her fault.

She understood this intellectually, but it was difficult to feel it emotionally. Her feelings simply would not catch up with what she believed.

When she finally began to confront her past, her guilt turned to anger toward men in general and her father in particular. Sometimes just the texture of a piece of cloth or the sight of a certain room would trigger bitter memories. She wished she could have killed her father. This man, who claimed to be a fine Christian and was respected in the community, this man who should have protected her, actually destroyed her.

She viewed herself as unattractive, and in honesty had to admit that she was ashamed of her body. Physical symptoms of her emotional pain began to surface — backaches, neck pain, insomnia, and nightmares. Eating disorders also began.

She found herself preferring to be alone. She shunned most male companionship, not only fearing to be touched but also fearing that some man might actually fall in love with her. If that were to happen, she would have the uncomfortable assignment of dealing with a relationship she did not care to have. She wanted to maintain her emotional space, so she set up boundaries that she did not intend for anyone to violate. Emotional distance could be most easily controlled by controlling physical distance. Her circle of friends grew small.

She could think of God only as the Creator. Surely He was not a heavenly Father. Where was He during those years of incest? She had prayed for the abuse to stop, but God did not intervene. Why should He be trusted now? Like her earthly father, her heavenly Father had betrayed her.

Only one thing kept her emotionally afloat during those dark days of anger and doubt. She had a few Christian friends who accepted her *no matter what*. She believed that they would not lie to her. When they said God could be trusted she accepted the fact that they believed this; it was true for them even if it was not true for her. Occasionally they would read Scripture with her, but they would not force her to believe. Doubt, they pointed out, was often a part of our experience with God. Just consider David's days of questioning as given in the psalms.

Yet in the midst of the gloom, something imperceptible was happening. Susan was coming to grips with her dormant past. After years of denial, she finally was confronting the enemy. Because she admitted what had happened, she could pinpoint the source of her problems. That was half the battle. The other half was to know how to handle her feelings now that the secret was out. Fortunately, because of Christ, this story has a happy ending.

Susan has learned how to put her past behind her. This barrier, now conquered, has become for her a stepping stone. She has found satisfaction in helping numerous others with similar backgrounds. Her life is proof that there is hope for those who have experienced sexual and physical abuse.

How was Susan helped in her struggle for emotional wholeness? Today she gives us the keys that opened the way for her to put her past behind her.

First, *her friends believed her story.*

Why is this important? She is convinced there are many people who suffer from physical, emotional and sexual abuse who refuse to share their past with others for fear they will not be believed. Many suffer through their lives in quiet emotional pain. They fear that even if their story is believed, they will experience rejection once more. Susan's friends understood her reluctance. They trusted her, and eventually she could trust them.

It is important that friends of abuse victims understand the need for the victims to tell their story again and again. They have thought about it for many years; it has been the unconscious focus of their thoughts since childhood. The facts can be told in a few minutes but the emotional pain may linger for months or even years. The process of healing cannot be hurried along. Susan's friends didn't pry into her background but only listened intently to as much as she wanted to tell them. The story came out in bits and pieces over a period of time.

Second, *her friends kept assuring her that what had happened was not her fault.*

They reminded her that she was neither dirty nor bad. God was not condemning her. The guilt and shame had been forced on her by someone else, and that person would be accountable to God for his actions.

Her friends also kept the conversations confidential. Today Susan speaks candidly of her past, but it has not always been that way. During the first few months when she chose to talk to her friends about it, she cherished the assurance that she would be accepted and loved despite her experiences. She also needed to know that other people whom she did not know as well, or whom she felt she could not trust, would not find out. To trust a few selected friends is one thing; to trust mere acquaintances is quite another.

Her friends also respected her desire to shun physical contact. They befriended her, knowing that she did not want to be hugged or even gently touched.

Third, *Susan chose to forgive her father.*

Her anger toward her heavenly Father did not subside until she made peace with her earthly father.

There is no one formula that works for all survivors. Susan did have the opportunity of meeting with her father as an act of reconciliation before his death, but she did not want to discuss his past failures, not knowing how he would react. Would he admit to her what had happened? Could he stand the emotional pain that would come with a confession? Since he did not bring up the matter, she chose not to. As for her attitude toward him, the anger was gone. She at least could let her father depart in peace.

Today Susan is frequently asked whether victims of abuse should confront the abuser. Some think it is necessary to do so. Unfortunately, this often results in more rejection and hurt because 80 percent of those confronted deny they did anything wrong. Such a response only aggravates the anger of the victim. We must admit realistically that many people who have hardened their hearts (as any unrepentant abuser must do) are simply incapable of seeing themselves for what they are. In many cases, reconciliation in this life is impossible.

How then can a person release the feelings of anger? Susan recommends you write a letter to the one who victimized you, and then choose not to send it. Or pretend that the person is seated in an empty chair while you say everything you would like to if he or she were actually present. Perhaps a friend can play the role of your parent or relative so that you can receive a sympathetic ear.

Don't be discouraged if the feelings of anger or shame return repeatedly. It is not uncommon to hear some people say it took them months or even years to fully lay down the anger and betrayal they felt.

Meanwhile God is capable of handling your anger and doubt. He is not waiting to clobber us just because we cannot understand His ways. Job experienced a trial that made him rethink his entire concept of God. It is the same for those who have experienced the deep hurt of abuse.

Keep in mind the principle of the ultimate justice of God. No one will ever get by with anything. The sins inflicted on others will be cared for by the sacrifice of Christ, or else the offender will bear them in his own person forever. Either way, justice will be fully satisfied.

Remember, you can choose how the abuse will affect your life. How tragic it would have been if Susan had allowed her father to continue to ruin her future. Had he not already done enough damage? Must his influence have continued even after his death?

Unfortunately, some people continue to hang on to the offense rather than releasing their bitterness in the presence of God.

Susan chose the better way.

> Let all bitterness and wrath and anger and clamor and slander be put away from you, along with all malice. And be kind to one another, tender-hearted, forgiving each other, just as God in Christ also has forgiven you (Ephesians 4:31,32).

10

SEXUAL ADDICTION:
A Personal Testimony

*Understanding and recovering
from sexual addiction*

TED WAS TWELVE when his older brother introduced him to pornography. He quickly became "hooked" on it, and this habit led him to a life of immorality. In ever-increasing ways, Ted went from one partner to another.

He was married at age 22, but the vows he took to "love, honor and cherish" were broken within three weeks of the wedding. Of course, he tried to keep his infidelity hidden. He skillfully arranged his schedule and, when necessary, lied about his whereabouts. By the time his first child was born, his wife Christine began to suspect that Ted was being unfaithful. She feared to confront him until one day, in the heat of an argument, she hurled the accusation in his face. Like most adulterers, he vehemently denied the charge and went through a "how-can-I-love-you-when-you-don't-trust-me" routine.

Ted was a Christian, and so was his wife. The natural guilt that accompanies all immorality was intensified by the knowledge that he was grieving the Holy Spirit, but Ted decided to play the religious game while he continued an affair on the side. In church he appeared friendly toward other believers and relatively enthusiastic about his commitment to Christ. In Sunday school he often was the one with the right answer. No one could possibly have guessed what lay beneath the surface.

Finally one day Christine discovered incontrovertible evidence that Ted was involved with another woman. At first Ted admitted only that he was friends with the woman, denying sexual involvement. Only when the evidence mounted did he agree that yes, he was guilty. But the relationship, he said, was fleeting; Christine could be sure it would not happen again. He also denied that he had been involved with other women.

To make a long story short, Ted continued his sinful liaisons. When this came to the attention of the elders of the church, he lied, then hedged, and finally admitted his guilt, tearfully showing repentance and seeking restoration. He was given another chance, then another. Each time the cycle was the same: He would commit sexual sin, then tearfully promise he would change, only to do it again.

Was there a way out of Ted's vicious cycle, his continuing enslavement to sexual addiction? Yes, there was. The Savior who came to set His people free stands ready to deliver even those who have been under the control of impure relationships.

Believe it or not, Ted's marriage survived those sinful encounters. True, a lesser woman might have given up long ago, but Christine did not. She kept believing, praying and working—and it paid off.

What are the steps necessary for such a deliverance? It's important to understand that, although this was Ted's experience, what he had to learn applies to others as well who are in similar circumstances.

First, Ted had to *be honest*.

For him, this was a difficult step; he had lied for so long. Whenever he was caught, he admitted only to what others knew, steadfastly denying whatever he could. He talked about how he loved the Lord and his wife. He tried to make his sin look rather excusable if seen in the whole context of his life. His weeping generated sympathy.

This deceit continued to give Satan a strong hold on his life. Ted had, in effect, dropped the breastplate of righteousness, thus opening himself to repeated exploitation by demonic powers. When he finally decided to swallow his pride and come clean, he felt relieved for the first time in years. The breastplate of righteousness could begin to deflect Satan's darts once again.

Besides lying to cover his sin, Ted also had become a skillful manipulator. He knew how to cry, admit how bad he was, shift the blame to his wife, and get others to sympathize with him. That's why his repentance and promises were of no avail. With the new honesty, all that had to change.

Second, he had to *understand the nature of true repentance*.

It was not just that he had to confess the sin of the past. He had to yield himself fully to God for the future. One of the reasons he had not told the whole story before was that he knew his friends would hold him accountable; in the past, he wanted to keep his options open.

In total surrender to God, Ted was completely honest with his friends. He told of his continuing secret use of pornography, and he decided to put this sin behind him forever. He realized there could be no compromise with the lusts that had enslaved him.

Somewhere I read a story about a man who sold his house to a client, but demanded that he (the original owner) be permitted to own one nail that was partially protruding near the front door. After the deal was finished, the original owner hung decayed meat on that nail. It could not be removed since that would have violated the agreement. The new owner eventually had to move out because the odor permeated the whole house! Ted was learning that when even the smallest sin is tolerated, it will take over, or permeate, a man's whole life.

Third, Ted had to *understand some things about the nature of sexual sin and why it can be repeated so easily.*

Paul says:

> Do you not know that the one who joins himself to a harlot is one body with her? For He says, "The two will become one flesh" (1 Corinthians 6:16).

Think of the implications: Ted had become one with each of the many women with whom he had shared a bed. This "oneness" was meant to be experienced with only one woman, his wife. Numerous relationships brought guilt, distractions and confusion. Once having committed the sin, it was easy to repeat it.

Ted had to renounce and confess his immoral behavior. His current mistress was told that the relationship was over forever. The power of Ted's memories would have to be overcome with prayer.

Fourth, he had to *see both how deeply he had wounded his wife and how critical it was to rebuild their relationship.*

Christine was able to accept her husband when he finally became honest with her. One night they talked and wept until 3 A.M., sharing their struggles as they should have been doing for years.

Fifth, he needed to *put huge amounts of the Word of God into his mind every day.*

From then on he had to think of himself differently. He was no longer the helpless adulterer, the defeated slave to sensuality. He would have to claim His position in Christ—he was forgiven and cleansed, and he was an heir of God and a joint-heir with Christ. The mind of the flesh had to be transformed into the mind of the Spirit.

This faith did not come easily. He began by reading a lot of Scripture and memorizing one verse each day. This discipline brought him into direct contact with spiritual struggles, the fiery darts of Satan. He learned how to pray warfare prayers and rebuke Satan in Christ's name. He learned, too, that he could not do that alone, but needed the persistent support of his Christian friends. Each week, he gave an honest account to them of his victories and defeats. Progress, though slow and unsteady, was made.

Finally, he had to *understand that this temptation would return.*

Because of his past life, he could easily fall when the opportunity arose. Perhaps one of Ted's most important decisions was to share openly with the friends who were committed to his restoration.

Homer in his Odyssey tells of the hero Odysseus who knew he would face incredible temptation when sailing near some beautiful semi-goddesses. The goddesses sang with such entrancing voices that they lured the passing sailors to their doom by running their ships aground on the sharp rocks nearby.

Odysseus had his men tie him up with the order that they not let him loose no matter how much he begged them. He even poured wax in their ears so the men would not hear his cries. Soon the enchanting music of the goddesses reached him, and he signaled frantically to be freed from his bonds. His men refused, and they sailed safely by.

For those who find any temptation overwhelming, it is necessary to be completely committed to others who can help as they sail through dangerous waters. When the Romans went to war, it was with beveled shields that could be interlocked. The advancing army moved like a wall against the enemy. This image was in Paul's mind when he spoke of "taking up the shield of faith with which you will be able to extinguish all the flaming missiles of the evil one" (Ephesians 6:16).

Linked together, believers are invincible in their struggle against Satan. No addiction can match the power of the Holy Spirit unleashed in a believing church. Yet we must guard each victory, knowing that the enemy is always waiting to reclaim lost ground.

11

ALCOHOLISM:
A Personal Testimony

*Christ has not promised to heal all
sickness, but He can deliver from all sin*

THE EARLIEST MEMORIES that Dan has
etched in his mind are scenes of insecurity and fear.
His parents fought constantly; his father would slap
his mother's face or push her against the wall.

His father was an alcoholic but refused to
admit his addiction. He drifted from job to job, cursing
his predicament and vowing war on the world. When
Dan was ten his parents divorced.

Sometimes children of an alcoholic father
develop such a hatred for drink they refuse to touch it,
but Dan followed in his father's footsteps. By the time
he reached his early teens he was getting drunk on
weekends but was convincing himself he was firmly in
control of this habit.

When he was 22, he was introduced to the
gospel through a Christian friend at the university.

Dan began attending a Bible study, quit drinking regularly and intended to live a dedicated Christian life.

Two years later he married a fine Christian woman, Marylin, who knew that her husband drank occasionally, but was satisfied that his social drinking was harmless. However, these small steps in a wrong direction eventually drove him deeper into sin. Dan learned that disobedience has bitter rewards.

Within a year of their marriage, a crisis developed. Dan was unemployed and Marylin had a miscarriage; later she spent a month in the hospital after emergency surgery. Dan became depressed and angry with God because of the series of tragedies that threatened their fledgling relationship. Increasingly, he turned to drink. In his sober moments he realized his life was following the same path as that of his father. Arguments, physical abuse and financial pressures eventually led to an eruption. Marylin threatened to file for divorce but the birth of their first child halted her plans.

Dan promised he would quit drinking in order to save the marriage, but Marylin was skeptical. She remembered the many times he promised he would never take another drink, only to be drunk by nightfall. Whenever she broached the subject, Dan bristled, denying he was an alcoholic. Sometimes he would go without drinking for a whole weekend, and this, in his mind, proved he was not addicted. Even when he was fired for being drunk on the job, he steadfastly refused to admit he had a problem. It was the boss's fault, or the company's fault, or even the family's fault.

Though Dan drifted from job to job, he always seemed to have money for drink although his children had few clothes and little to eat. He would find excuses to "borrow" money, saying it was needed to pay the rent, buy groceries or pay for unexpected medical expenses. He borrowed money from one friend to pay another as his debts mounted. His guilt drove him to more drink, which in turn drove him further into debt, and thus increased his guilt.

A crisis brought him to his senses. One weekend, after he had received a refund from the IRS, he drank so heavily his wife had to call an ambulance to take him to the hospital. There he spent several terrifying days of withdrawal, accompanied by hallucinations and nightmares. By the time he had regained his senses, he finally admitted to his wife that he had a problem, and he was willing to do whatever was necessary for him to be free.

There in the hospital, Dan turned to the Christ he had accepted as a young man. Faced with a problem that was too big for him to handle, he cast himself upon the mercy of God in Christ. For the first time in years, he had a sense of release and peace. Christ finally had all of him.

The **first** step toward his recovery was *his own humble acknowledgment that he was no longer in control*. The denials and the lies had to give way to the stark reality that he was bound by a sinful habit and needed help to get out.

"He . . . gives grace to the humble." Submit therefore to God. Resist the devil and he will flee from you (James 4:6,7).

Second, along with this new attitude, Dan began *to admit he could no longer blame others for his problems*. He had looked at life from the point of view of a typical alcoholic: He saw his wife and children as his enemies. After all, it was their need for clothes and food that so often stood in the way of him and his precious bottle. For the first time now, he actually could see this addiction as his fault. He felt guilty when he thought of what he had been doing to his wife and family. Now he took the blame and allowed it to rest squarely on his own shoulders.

This was a crucial moment of insight. Those hooked on some sin of the flesh find it nearly impossible to see themselves as they are. Alcoholics, in particular, find reality so unbearable that they will choose any irrational explanation for their problems rather than a rational one. Anything is better than the frightening truth.

Today much teaching about alcoholism places the blame on chemistry, on one's heritage, or on the environment. Yet the Bible teaches that the sin of drunkenness is a product of the flesh, just as other sins are. Christ won a victory over all the sins listed, whether sorcery, anger, envy or drunkenness (Galatians 5:20,21). As we noted earlier, Christ has not promised to heal all of our sicknesses, but He is able to deliver us from all of our sins. Calling alcoholism by its right name is an important step on the path of victory.

Finally, Dan was willing to admit he needed accountability. No longer could he go it alone. His hidden sin would have to be admitted. He would need a group of friends who would steer him away from drink rather than toward it. Although he had not made friends within the church, he was willing to join with some men in a Bible study and develop relationships that would help keep him from the vicious cycle. Admitting his addiction was difficult, but he had little choice. If he wanted out, his sin could be hidden no longer.

This, incidentally, explains why the Alcoholics Anonymous organization has been so successful. A group of men or women band together to hold one another accountable for their actions. They are committed to the positive peer pressure that comes as a result of the friendships formed with those who face similar struggles. This, of course, is a biblical principle:

We can fight our enemies more successfully together than we can alone.

This is true even among non-Christians.

Dan had the added benefit of knowing the living Christ. He joined a Bible study with Christians to whom he acknowledged his need. They prayed for him and agreed they would hold him accountable. He would have to share honestly how he was doing in the Christian life.

The New Testament teaches it is not normally possible to experience the victory of Christ unless it is done in fellowship with other Christians.

Listen to Colossians 2:2:

> That their hearts may be encouraged, having been knit together in love, and attaining to all the wealth that comes from the full assurance of understanding, resulting in a true knowledge of God's mystery, that is, Christ Himself.

In the meantime, Marylin was receiving some wise counsel from her pastor, who told her she must no longer be her husband's crutch—for example, making excuses for him when he was too drunk to go to work. She would have to cooperate with the process by helping him face reality, no matter how cruel that seemed to be. And they would have to make restitution for the lies of the past.

For three months Dan remained sober. One day he was at a gathering of business associates and was invited to take a drink. His long period of sobriety gave him the confidence that he could take just one drink and stop. That day, he did. This added to his sense of accomplishment; he had indeed conquered the problem, he thought. He could drink and quit whenever he wanted to. This attitude set him up for his greatest fall.

One weekend when his wife was at a women's seminar, Dan decided to stop by the tavern just as he had in days gone past. He was confident his addiction was behind him; he had proven it to himself. But on this day, the first glass started him on a binge that did not end until far into the night. When his wife returned home, she found him sprawled on the floor.

Dan learned by experience what he had been told many times: He would be susceptible to alcohol for the rest of his life. Alcoholics Anonymous teaches that even those who have been sober for ten years should remind themselves each day, "I am an alcoholic."

Dan learned we can never compromise with the desires of the flesh. Christ warned, "Truly, truly, I say to you, everyone who commits sin is the slave of sin" (John 8:34). Christ's point is that whenever we choose to sin, the consequences of that decision are taken out of our hands. To sin deliberately is to enter into an agreement with an enemy who is stronger than we are. We voluntarily put ourselves under the authority of a tyrant. Our decision to walk into a trap may be voluntary, but our decision to walk out is not. To extricate ourselves from the grip of the enemy, we need outside help.

Fortunately, Dan is sober today and his marriage is doing well. He is living proof that there can be life in spite of alcoholism. Jesus said the enemy can plunder our lives only until we have a friend who is stronger than the enemy is. "The slave does not remain in the house forever; the son does remain forever. If therefore the Son shall make you free, you shall be free indeed" (John 8:35,36).

There is no alcoholic who cannot be free. The price is repentance, honesty with others and accountability. Christ is standing beside those who are struggling, ready to give a hand to them when they are desperate enough to give the control of their lives over to Him. With God, all things are possible.

12

HOMOSEXUALITY:
A Personal Testimony

*You can come to God on your own, just
as you are, and He will welcome you*

AT THE AGE OF SIX Roger Montgomery
was molested by a homosexual neighbor, and that
introduced him to the homosexual lifestyle. Roger
continued to be molested with some degree of regu-
larity during the next six years.

These experiences were painful at first, but
the neighbor befriended Roger and the boy began to
like him, so over a period of years he began to enjoy the
relationship. He apparently gravitated toward the man
because he did not have a close relationship with
anyone else.

Roger's parents kept pornography in their
home and this inflamed Roger's sexual desires. His
father was interested in looking at women, and his
mother bought pornography that glorified the male
body. Roger was attracted to that. He soon realized
that he had no attraction toward women, only toward
men.

As he grew up he had other sexual contacts with young men his own age. Bothered by his homosexuality, he thought he could overcome it if he attended a Christian Bible college. He thought that if he worked hard to crucify the flesh, he could make himself worthy enough for God to accept. It didn't work. During the first year at college he became sexually involved with his roommate, and as he continued with pornography on his own, his desires became stronger and stronger. He finally concluded he was incapable of changing himself. His desires were stronger than he was.

Expelled from the Bible school, he became increasingly bitter toward God. One evening he looked up into the sky and vehemently cursed Him, telling Him that He was weak, He was a liar and that He could not help him. Roger hated God for what He did.

The day he cursed God, his life began to fall apart. He soon became homeless and unable to hold a job. His sexual appetite was so strong he would be out late every night pursuing various relationships. He didn't get enough sleep and so wasn't able to get to work in the morning. He practically lived in gay bars, entering when they opened and staying until they closed. On drugs by this time, he eventually got into prostitution to support himself and his drug habit. Totally immersed in his world of perverted sex, he had no time in his life for anything except feeding his addiction.

Now that he had shut God out of his life, he was really having a "good time." Then the AIDS virus came to America. It was inevitable after so many contacts (he'd had more than a thousand sexual partners) that he would contract the virus. He began to fear death, so he began to think about God again—though not too seriously, because, he told himself, he had tried God before and it had not worked. God had refused to help him. At the same time, Roger realized nothing else in his life was working either— he was in a big mess and on the verge of suicide.

He said, "You must understand how deeply I was driven by lust. I would have several homosexual encounters in a single evening. Some homosexuals have ten or twenty relationships in one night." He went on to describe mass orgies in bathhouses and similar places. Then he added, "Many homosexuals will laugh when I say this, but I know now that in my experience, I was empowered by Satan. I did not have the physical capacity to do what I did—I had a driving, evil force within me, overpowering me, and I had no control over my life or my thoughts. After ten or so encounters at night, I would wake up the next morning wondering where I could find my next partner."

After so many years of living on the street and engaging in various kinds of sex, he felt dirty. He had alienated his family, and he had no friends. Nowhere to turn. And God seemed so distant.

Yet God continued to work in Roger's heart. Roger began to understand his mistake: He'd thought he had to change before God would accept him. Somehow he never had realized that he could come to God as he was—as a homosexual—and that God would welcome him into His family.

Years earlier Roger thought he had understood the gospel. Now God seemed to be asking him if he really believed that if he were willing to repent of his homosexuality, God would make him into a new creature even though he continued to have the desires of a homosexual. It was as if God were asking him simply, "Do you believe the gospel?"

His part was to come to Christ acknowledging his need, and God would do the rest. So he said, "Yes, I do." That was the beginning of his deliverance from homosexuality.

He said, "The greatest day of my life was when I realized that all I had to do was believe and I could trust Christ for the rest."

God did not work on Roger's sexuality at all in the beginning, though. He dealt first with many other sins: pride, anger, rebellion, hostility toward his parents, etc. Roger kept asking, "God, when are You going to get to the issue of my homosexuality?"

Only after a series of victories in other areas of Roger's life did God finally begin to deliver him from the homosexuality. God had to bring Roger to the point where he was willing to accept the responsibility for his own condition.

He had always rationalized his lifestyle, saying, "Well, look what this man did to me when I was six years old, and think of what my parents did." God did not deliver him until he accepted the fact that he alone was answerable for the decisions he made. "Even though I was a sinner in Adam, I was still responsible for my own actions. Only when I took ownership was I able to give my homosexuality to Christ. As long as it was 'somebody else's problem,' there was no way He could forgive me and deliver me."

Nearly two years passed before Roger's transformation to heterosexuality was complete. The sin in his life did not just disappear as soon as he was saved. Fortunately, he was able to share his testimony with a pastor who befriended him and spent time discipling him.

Relinquishing his bitterness against God was the major breakthrough God used to bring Roger's deliverance. "I believe one of the things that kept me trapped in homosexuality during my teenage years is the lie that a person is born a homosexual. I also heard repeatedly that it is impossible for homosexuals to change. Needless to say, I felt I had no choice—like it or not, I was doomed to that lifestyle.

"Today I am convinced that no one is born a homosexual. I had from 1000 to 1500 different relationships, and I often asked my partners how they got into homosexuality. It was a favorite topic because they like to talk about their companions and experiences. By far the majority said they had been molested as children; they had been recruited by a neighbor, friend or relative. Usually this was accompanied by the use of pornography."

After Roger was saved, the temptations were incredible; opportunities for sexual experiences were everywhere. He lived in the suburbs and took the train downtown to his work as a clerk. Every day the train went right through the gay area, and Roger was sorely tempted to go back to his former lifestyle. He said, "It was not will power that kept me during those days, because I was very weak spiritually. I can only attribute it to a miracle of Christ."

Over and over it was as if God were asking, "Do you believe? Do you trust Me?"

Roger kept saying, "Yes, Lord. I believe in You and I want to follow You, because that is the right way."

Sometimes he would call his pastor from work and say, "I am really tempted to go to a gay bar today."

The pastor would respond, "No. I'll meet you downtown in 20 minutes, and I'll go home with you." He didn't know the answers to all of Roger's problems, but he was there to help when Roger needed him.

Roger also had some quality Christian friends who helped him during those difficult days, but he had to learn on his own, through study and meditation in the Scriptures, how to resist temptation.

Roger wanted others to understand the transformation that God wrought in his life. As a homosexual he had hated women, not just sexually, but as people. Though he was often around them (particularly in high school), the thought of heterosexual relationships repulsed him. After he was saved he met two former lesbians who were attending the same church he was and they became close friends.

God did not substitute heterosexual lust for homosexual lust, so Roger was not attracted to every woman he met, but he did enjoy being with women then, and was neither afraid of them nor intimidated by them.

A while later he met another woman, who was "straight," and she and Roger served the Lord together in a nursing home. They soon fell in love and were married.

During his days as a homosexual he often had walked past churches, thinking maybe somebody would give him hope, because he was a hopeless person. No one invited him in, but he was glad he finally realized he could come to Christ on his own and that homosexuality is really no different from any other sin such as lying, cheating, etc. Yes, the addiction is stronger, but Christ can overcome it.

He found, however, that many homosexuals are content and do not want to change. Only when they are off alcohol and sex for a few days do they become miserable. As long as they can satisfy their addictions they are happy. Roger began to reach out to homosexuals, challenging them to think again about what God says regarding homosexuality. He pleaded with them to rethink their beliefs in the Bible, and to trust Christ for forgiveness and a new life.

Facing death was especially sobering for Roger. Though he was now a Christian and ready to die, he often wondered if anyone is ever really ready to stand in God's presence. He constantly asked himself, *What am I doing for Christ? Am I who Christ wants me to be? Am I using today for the glory of God?*

He didn't look forward to the suffering of AIDS, but sometimes he lay awake at night rejoicing that he would be with the Lord soon. He related, "This strange joy and peace comes over me—and that is what gets me through every day. I don't spend my day saying, 'Lord, I'm going to die of AIDS. Can You heal me?' I do pray for healing, but that is not the main thing in my life. I want to live every day for Christ, and I pray for His soon return."

Roger Montgomery died of AIDS on November 6, 1989. The organization he founded to help homosexuals, called New Creation,* continues under the leadership of his wife Rene.

Roger's parting comment was this: "If heterosexuals go to the homosexual community and say, 'We want you to change,' they are carrying the wrong message. We should tell them that what they are doing is a sin and, if they are willing to admit that and come to Christ, they will be forgiven and accepted by God."

* For more information about this organization, write:
New Creation Ministries
P. O. Box 2663
Paducah, KY 42002

13

GOODBYE TO THE PAST

There is hope for everyone

A TEENAGE GIRL found her father in the bushes, dead from a self-inflicted gunshot wound. She spent the next several years in therapy, trying desperately to put her life back together. It was not just her father's suicide that kept her on the verge of a nervous breakdown but also the pain of rejection she had experienced while growing up. Her parents had divorced, and her mother had abandoned the home. The father then had abused his daughter often, lashing out in anger. She vividly remembers being pushed down the stairs and into the street to fend for herself.

After years of emotional paralysis she is now able to live a normal life because she has come to understand the acceptance of Christ and the reality of the love of God. She is comforted by the knowledge that Christ saw what happened to her as a girl and that He loved her through all the pains of life. She discovered that Christ helps an individual come to terms with a past that cannot be changed. Eventually she married and is now happily adjusted.

Some people are more successful than others in putting their past behind them. Two individuals may have similar backgrounds of abuse or immorality, and one may be able to go on to live a fulfilled life while the other may not be able to close the door to the past.

There is no easy explanation for these differences. By nature some people are more sensitive than others and cannot seem to let go of the pain. Others take their hurts in stride and simply refuse to be controlled by them. Despite past tragedy and sin, today they live emotionally stable and productive lives. No wonder Paul referred to our Lord as "the God of hope."

The cross of Christ is central to all emotional healing. The fact that Christ bore our sins there is well known; what is often overlooked is that He bore our emotional burdens as well.

Surely our griefs He Himself bore,
And our sorrows He carried . . . (Isaiah 53:4).

Here is hope for those whose emotions have been crushed by a troubled past.

Perhaps one reason some people recover more fully from a painful past is they have the settled conviction that God is greater than anything they have ever experienced. To quote Corrie Ten Boom, "There is no pit so deep but that God is deeper still."

The cross gives hope for several reasons. **First,** there is *forgiveness for past sins.*

Thus a young woman who has had an abortion can be freed from the emotional trauma of guilt that comes with killing her unborn child. Recently I heard of a woman who had aborted a child who actually experienced a manifestation of an evil spirit posing as the child to bring accusations against her. The guilt drove her to the brink of insanity. Her rescue came only when she admitted she had murdered her baby, and received God's forgiveness for it. Yes, the cross can wipe out the accusing finger of the past.

Second, the cross can bring *peace despite past injustices and turbulence.*

Christ gives us the courage we need to face our hurts honestly. Knowing our relationship with God is secure, we can begin to probe the depths of our feelings without the fear of confronting something that is too much for God. Whatever hurt we may uncover, God can give us the grace to cope with it successfully. Think of the cross as an exchange: Christ takes our sin and sorrows and gives us His love and acceptance.

When the Israelites came to Marah they were deeply disappointed because they could not drink the bitter water. Yet when Moses found a tree and threw it into the water, the water became sweet. A miracle? Yes. A picture of the miraculous power of the cross.

There are two important trees in the Bible: **One** is the tree of the knowledge of good and evil of which Adam and Eve ate. That tree was the means by which all of humanity became polluted. Its poison has affected every human being; thanks to that tree, we all have a past of some kind that must be laid to rest.

The **second** tree is the one on which Christ hung for us. This tree also brought a curse, for "Cursed is everyone who hangs on a tree" (Galatians 3:13). The difference is that through this tree the bitter waters were made sweet; life with all of its hurts became bearable.

When Christ was on the cross He was offered wine mingled with gall (myrrh, from which came the word *marah)* to lessen His pain. He refused it. The cup of bitterness He drank for us would be without mixture.

Today the world offers a variety of trees, promising they will make bitter waters sweet. Riches, pleasure, alcohol—these and a host of other remedies are prescribed to help people get through one more day. In the end, these only make the waters more bitter and poisonous.

Christ sweetens everything He touches, sometimes using our failures more productively than our successes. Sometimes the bitter oasis rather than the sweet
one reveals God's finest gifts.

Third, the cross of Christ gives us hope as we
apply it to our lives by remembering that *Satan received a
mortal wound when Christ died.*

Christ proved once for all that after Satan has his
day, God has His. Joy follows pain. All of Satan's work
eventually will serve the higher purposes of God. The best
Satan was able to do was nip Christ's heel; Christ in turn
crushed Satan's head.

Not a one of God's children can receive a mortal
wound. They are severely wounded, yes, but they are not
crushed. The flower will bloom; the sun will shine. The
destructive influences of an abusive family and our own
failures can be broken. Through the intercession of other
believers, we can take authority over the sins of the past.
It may take prayer and fasting, but God will honor His
promises.

Fourth, the cross is a *reminder of the incredible
worth of a human being.*

Initially we derive our sense of self-worth from
our parents. If they love and accept us, we conclude we are
valuable and life is worth living. Those who have not felt
the love of parents, or who have been hated from birth,
often suffer from depression, aimlessness and inability to
show love. Some harden their hearts and withdraw, determined never to try to love or be loved again. Others act out
their sense of worthlessness by filling their lives with
immorality, drugs or crime. Yet, for everyone there is hope.

Have you ever thought how wonderful it would
have been to be a child of Mary and Joseph, and thus a
half-brother of the Lord? Christ made a startling comment
to some people who were telling him His relatives were
outside. He asked, "Who are My mother and My brothers?

. . . Whosoever does the will of God, he is My brother and sister and mother" (Mark 3:33,34).

We have the privilege of being His mother, brother and sister! We might think He would be embarrassed to stoop low enough to count us as members of His own family. Yet we read, "He is not ashamed to call" us brothers (Hebrews 2:11).

Christ taught that the Father loves us just as much as He loves the Son; the Father is just as interested in our lives as He was in Christ's. We are accepted in the beloved one.

Finally, the cross *unites us with other believers who can help* us in our times of physical and spiritual hurt.

When we are in an emotional rut that is both deep and crooked, we need one of Christ's representatives to pull us out and to bring us from despair to hope.

My friend, are you willing to let God love you? Will you stop trying to get God to accept you on the basis of your performance? Will you remember that there is a rest for the people of God—a rest for those who trust wholly in God's promises? As He spoke to the storm on Galilee, He can speak a word of peace to any raging heart.

This does not mean we will always live with emotional tranquillity. Indeed, even Christ Himself experienced sharp pangs of grief at Gethsemane. It does mean, however, that we will always have the resources to cope; we will be able to do what is right.

You may never experience all of the emotional fulfillment you would like, but God will make up for that in other ways. In fact, those "other ways" may be the goal God has in mind for you.

> Why are you so downcast, O my soul?
>   Why are you so disturbed within me?
> Put your hope in God,
>   for I will yet praise Him,
>   my Savior and my God (Psalm 42:5, NIV).

Reference Notes

Chapter 2

1. William Justice, *Guilt and Forgiveness* (Grand Rapids: Baker Book House, n.d.), p. 105.
2. Ibid., p. 95.
3. *Decision* (January 1990), p. 12.

Chapter 3

1. John Piper, ((NEED BOOK OR ARTICLE TITLE, PUBLISHER AND DATE--& P. #S IF POSSIBLE?????)))

Chapter 4

1. Cheryl Lavin, "Guilty of Adultery," *Chicago Tribune* (September 13, 1989).
2. Richard Brzeczek, *Addicted to Adultery: How We Saved Our Marriage/How You Can Save Yours* (New York: Bantam Books, 1989).
3. Patrick Carnes, *Out of the Shadows: Understanding Sexual Addiction* (Minneapolis: CompCare, 1985), p. 64.

Chapter 5

1. David Seamands, *The Healing of Memories* (Wheaton, IL: Victor Books, 1985).

Chapter 6

1. This description of the four stages of demonic control is taken from the booklet, *Coming to Grips With Satan's Plan for Your Life*, by Erwin W. Lutzer (Chicago: Moody Press, 1990).

Chapter 7

1. Mark Bubeck, *The Adversary* (Chicago: Moody Press, 1975). See pp. 74-77 for entire prayer.
2. Ibid, pp. 106-7.